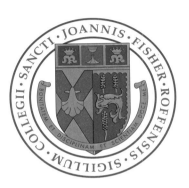

Lavery Library

St. John Fisher
College
Rochester, New York

Samuel Beckett
Anatomy of a Literary Revolution

Samuel Beckett
Anatomy of a Literary Revolution

Pascale Casanova

Translated by Gregory Elliott

VERSO
London • New York

Liberté • Égalité • Fraternité
RÉPUBLIQUE FRANÇAISE

This book is supported by the French Ministry of Foreign Affairs as part of the Burgess programme run by the Cultural Department of the French Embassy in London. (www.frenchbooknews.com)

This edition published by Verso 2006
© Verso 2006
Translation © Gregory Elliott 2006
Introduction © Terry Eagleton 2006
First published as *Beckett l'abstracteur. Anatomie d'une révolution littéraire*
© Editions du Seuil 1997

1 3 5 7 9 10 8 6 4 2

Verso
UK: 6 Meard Street, London W1F 0EG
USA: 180 Varick Street, New York, NY 10014-4606
www.versobooks.com

Verso is the imprint of New Left Books

ISBN-13: 978-1-84467-112-0
ISBN-10: 1-84467-112-7

British Library Cataloguing in Publication Data
A catalogue record for this book is available from the British Library

Library of Congress Cataloging-in-Publication Data
A catalog record for this book is available from the Library of Congress

Typeset in Bembo by Hewer Text UK Ltd, Edinburgh
Printed in the USA by Quebecor World

Introduction

by Terry Eagleton

Samuel Beckett is one of those writers about whom almost nobody nowadays has a bad word to say, despite the fact that the first London production of *Waiting for Godot* was greeted with outraged cries of 'This is how we lost the Empire!' Yet this well-nigh universal approval may not be entirely for the right reasons. Beckett's work is undoubtedly somewhat bleak for the taste of a middle class which has traditionally required its art to be edifying; but it seems on the other hand so exactly the kind of thing the middle class expects its modern art to be – namely, a tolerably obscure investigation of the 'human condition' – that its gloom may be largely forgiven. In any case, there are always critics on hand to scour these remorselessly negative texts for the occasional glimmer of humanistic hope, in a world where rank pessimism is felt to be somehow ideologically subversive.

Beckett's prose is so palpably 'universal', so packed with pregnant lines, half-symbols and cryptic allusions, and his drama is so much the sort of thing that the West End theatregoer confidently expects from his evening out, that one wonders whether this stark, gratifyingly 'deep' discourse of Man is not at some level as mischievously parodic as the work of his fellow Dubliner Oscar Wilde, who in poker-faced style turned out drawing-room dramas so impeccably well-made that they deferred to the English at the very moment they sent them up.

This existential-cum-metaphysical Beckett, resonant with the pathos of Being, may be a character dear to the heart of Maurice Blanchot, who figures more or less as the villain of this book; but it is far from the astonishingly revolutionary artist that Pascale Casanova presents us with here. This is a Beckett who pursues the logic of abstraction to its most inhuman extremes; who refuses the morphine of idealism even when in severe pain; whose work represents a merciless onslaught on the pretensions of Literature; and who preserves a compact with silence, breakdown and failure in the face of historical triumphalism and the self-flaunting word. As Casanova points out, he is out to dismantle the very conventional conditions of possibility of literature: 'the subject, memory, imagination, narration, character, psychology, space and time . . .' What else is his drama *Breath* but a response to the question: How can you write a play with no dialogue, scenery, plot, action or character? As for his 'world view', it is not out of the question that Beckett himself, despite his lugubrious oeuvre, might have been in private life a sentimental optimist with a Panglossian faith in human nature. We know enough of his life, in fact, to know that he was nothing of the kind; not many Panglossian optimists have landed up on the couch of the psychoanalyst Wilfred Bion. Yet it is worth keeping the possibility in mind, just to remind ourselves of this author's aversion to the idea that he was somehow 'expressing himself' in his writings. Even if anything as inconceivable as expression is going on, what is being expressed is certainly nothing as drearily passé as a self.

His work, in short, presents us with the scandal of a literature which no longer depends on a philosophy of the subject. The deflation of the rhetoric of achievement, along with the puristic horror of deceit which knows itself even so to be unavoidably mystified: this is no mere purveying of a 'way of seeing', but the stamp of a dissident, peripheral author who never ceases to shrink, mechanize and hack to the bone a twentieth-century world swollen with its own ideological bombast. It is no wonder he was such a fan of the evacuative aesthetics of his fellow Dubliner Jonathan Swift. For this politics of lessness, texts which only just manage to exist, statements which evaporate the very instant they flicker ambiguously up, break fewer bones than the declarations of a Jünger or a Heidegger. If Beckett was a great anti-fascist writer, it is not only because he fought with the French Resistance, a bravery for which he was awarded the *Croix de Guerre*, but because every sentence of his writing keeps faith with powerlessness. The sheer contingency of his prose cuts the ground from beneath the sense of destiny and absolute certitudes of his political enemy. Even his decision to write in French, as Casanova points out, was influenced by his sense that French represented 'a form of weakness' compared with the opulence of his native tongue.

This, as Adorno recognized, is partly a question of how to write after

Auschwitz. Yet it also belongs to a specifically Irish legacy. Like Heraclitus, the Irish have always held that nothing is quite as real as nothing. Medieval Irish theology, with its emphasis on the frailty and littleness of Jesus rather than the august majesty of God the Father, preserves a certain minimalist style, while the greatest of all Irish medieval philosophers, John Scotus Eriugena, was Europe's most subtle expounder of negative theology in the tradition of Pseudo-Dionysius, teaching the doctrine that God is non-being. Ireland's most eminent modern philosopher, George Berkeley, remarked that 'for us Irish, something and nothing are near allied', while his clerical colleague Archbishop King of Dublin wrote that 'all finite beings partake of nothing, and are nothing beyond their bounds'. The Tipperary-born novelist Laurence Sterne put in a word for nothingness, 'considering', he observed, 'what worse things there are in the world'. For the aesthetician Edmund Burke, as well as for the novelist Flann O'Brien, sublimity includes that which is barely visible as well as the immense and immeasurable, since both are equally ungraspable.

In modern times, these claims for the value of the negative, lowly or humbly unremarkable have a political resonance to them often enough. If Britain is very much something, then colonial Ireland is next to nothing. This inconsiderable afterthought of Europe, as Joyce scornfully dubbed it, was too small to give birth to the prodigal, capacious, ambitiously totalizing fictions of a Balzac or a Dickens. Instead, the short story became one of its most successful genres, pivoting as it does on a caught moment, isolated selfhood or stray epiphany. One of the nation's premier short story writers, Sean O'Faolain, felt that Ireland was too 'thin' a society, too lacking in 'complex social machinery', to be fit meat for novelistic fiction. Henry James thought something rather similar about his native United States. If Joyce produced a monstrous tome in *Ulysses*, it was as much as a parody of the English naturalistic novel as in homage to it. Wilde, who worked for the most part in minor genres, chose to dazzle the world as a major minor writer, while James Clarence Mangan left us with a clutch of poetic fragments and ruins.

Casanova's riposte to the Blanchot-ing of Beckett is to be both formal and historical in equal measure. This, at first glance, is a surprising combination of approaches, since we normally assume that historical criticism throws open a work to the winds of reality, while formalist techniques seek to seal it hermetically from them. Yet as Lukács reminded us, there is no more truly historical phenomenon in art than form, which is quite as much saturated in social signification as so-called content. And nothing is more historically eloquent than the moment when art comes either despairingly or triumphantly to claim its autonomy from history. There are those on the cultural left, half a century after Adorno did his work, who in their idealist fashion still regard aesthetic autonomy as simply a false way of perceiving artworks – as an ideological illusion rather than a material reality. The antidote to such misperception, so they imagine, is to historicize the work. But for one thing, historicizing, from Edmund Burke to Michael Oakeshott, has by no means always been the prerogative of the political left; and for another thing, form and aesthetic autonomy are historical phenomena in any case.

The story this study has to tell is not one of how Beckett's writing can be viewed both formally and historically, though its own combination of historical survey and close textual analysis is exemplary. It is rather the narrative of how this artist is forced into the embrace of avant-garde autonomy by virtue of a certain material history – one which is largely the history of his native Ireland. Let us take the question of autonomy first. Beckett's 'quasi-mathematical' art, as Casanova calls it, takes a set of postulates and in quasi-structuralist manner lets them run through their various permutations until the process is exhausted and another, equally rigorous, equally pointless computation takes over. Freed from social function, art can now unfurl its own inner logic. What other critics take to be portentous philosophical questions in Beckett – what? how? why? – Casanova boldly interprets as questions addressed by the texts to themselves, queries about their own procedures and conditions of possibility.

With small-nation perversity, Beckett's austerely Protestant texts set out to punish themselves by seeking to eke as many permutations as possible out of the scantiest number of component parts. Ingeniously reshuffling the same few poor scraps and leavings, they retain the ritual of Irish Catholicism while rebuffing its sensuous extravagance. A good deal of Irish writing (Synge and O'Casey, for example, or *Ulysses*) turns on an ironic contrast between the meagreness of the material and the elaborate stylizations of form; but in Beckett the only correspondence now left between words and things lies in their common destitution. There are some astute analyses of this method here, not least a 'redemptive' reading of the rather neglected *Worstward Ho*, which Casanova provocatively sees as the magisterial summation of its author's *ars combinatoria*.

As the study illustrates, this Dublin dissident was much taken with the thought of the minor Flemish Cartesian philosopher Geulincx, not least with his doctrine of the mutual autonomy of body and soul. In one sense, this leaves him firmly within the discourse of his own culture. The body as mechanism or automaton crops up in Irish writing all the way from Swift and Sterne to Flann O'Brien's sinisterly humanized bicycles. It is what happens to the flesh when it is forced in dire conditions to sever its consciousness from its materiality, so that the former becomes abstract and impotent, and the latter is reduced to so much meaningless, mechanical stuff. It is the contrast between Swift's Houyhnhnms and Yahoos, or Joyce's Stephen and Bloom. There is also something of this savage somatic reductionism in the work of the great Anglo-Irish painter Francis Bacon. 'When man acts, he is a puppet. When he describes, he is a poet', wrote Oscar Wilde. Men and women can transcend their barren material surroundings only in language, fantasy and imagination.

It is a familiar Irish theme, one which contrasts with the vein of Berkeleyan or Yeatsian idealism which sees the material world itself as a kind of spiritual discourse or divine semiosis. Materiality can either be cut off from the spirit or peremptorily reduced to it. Beckett retains an Irish carnivalesque preoccupation with the body – though it is a carnival turned sour, and what survives of the body is mostly its interminable suffering. Paradoxically, his dualism intensifies a sense of the world's recalcitrant bulk, rather than simply disembodying it. If he is a Cartesian rationalist, it is partly because such a doctrine shows up the poor forked creature humanity for what it is, rather than simply tidying its fleshliness out of sight. His texts present us with a world of brute objects and elusive meanings.

In another sense, however, Beckett's interest in this line of philosophical inquiry is one of several ways in which he cuts against the grain of Irish culture, since this impoverished country, deeply marked by religion and bereft of a robust bourgeoisie, gave birth to no major rationalism. Instead, from Eriugena to Berkeley, Yeats and beyond, its central philosophical current has been strongly idealist – a kind of secular competitor to religion, and one influenced in some cases by early Celtic spirituality.[1] What rationalists do crop up in Anglo-Irish writing, like Swift's Laputans and Sterne's Tristram Shandy, are satirical send-ups, as an excess of enlightenment capsizes into madness. Beckett's work, by contrast, is distinguished by a rationalist strain, which no doubt played a part in his attraction to France. No doubt it also plays a part in the French Pascale Casanova's attraction to him.

If this writer trades in ambiguities and indeterminacies, it is part of the irony of his work that he does so in a stringent, efficiently taxonomizing manner. What catches our eye, as Casanova pinpoints so admirably, is not the existential cloudiness or metaphysical portentousness of his writing, but its clear-eyed attempts at an exact formulation of the inarticulable, its monkish devotion to precision, the extreme scrupulousness with which it sculpts the void. In shaving ruthlessly away at the inessential, it reveals a Protestant animus against the superfluous and ornamental. It retains the fading forms of a zealous Protestant search for truth, even if it has scant faith in the truth itself. If it betrays a modernist scepticism of language, it combines it with a quasi-rationalist search for translucency. One might read this crazedly meticulous hair-splitting as a parody of Irish scholasticism, or as the ghost of a Protestant rationalism, or indeed as both.

As for the historical dimension, Casanova recounts with impressive concision the story of Beckett's fraught relations with the Irish Free State. Encircled by a parochial Gaelic bigotry, the Southern middle-class Protestant class into which Beckett was born had always felt themselves a besieged minority of cultural aliens. In Ireland, it was the rulers as much as the masses who felt dispossessed, which is why Yeats, Synge, Lady Gregory and Beckett had such fellow-feeling for vagrants. The Irish Literary Revival portrayed in this book was the eleventh-hour attempt of a liberal wing of the Anglo-Irish Ascendancy, a class which had been stripped of its economic base in the turn-of-the-century Land Acts, to enter into alliance with 'the people', thus substituting a form of cultural hegemony for the political leadership which as a class it had so signally failed to provide them with. Beckett, then, was an internal exile from birth, and like Synge and Wilde found a way of translating his displacement into a deeper fidelity to dispossession.

They also found a way to translate that displacement into a form of modernism. It is the sheer, uncompromising avant-gardeness of Beckett, his remorseless pursuit of a purely abstract literature, which comes through most powerfully in this book, not least in a sparkling discussion of his fascination with the paintings of the Van Velde brothers. In its distrust of psychological interiority and passion for the stylized and externalized, Beckett's theatre has an affinity with Brecht's. Casanova sees this break to cosmopolitan modernism, after a purgatorial period of paralysis, as part of Beckett's break with a claustrophobic native history, and this is surely the case. Yet having made the transition, he never ceases to look back and reinvent his native culture, exactly in the manner of his Parisian colleague Joyce. It is not only that sheer, *Godot*-like monotony is one of the qualities most regularly ascribed to everyday colonial life by nineteenth-century Irish writing, or that there may be a subliminal memory of Irish history in those barren, famished landscapes. It is also that no one tolerably familiar with Irish culture, not least with its debunkery, self-mockery, savagely ironic humour, carnivalesque strain, satire of pomposity, quick sense of farce and recurrent trope of bathos, can fail to find a distinctively Irish sensibility in these apparently disinherited texts. Above all, perhaps, Beckett remains Irish in his vein of mock-pedantry – the sign of a nation which values its lineages of high learning, but which cannot help playing them off sardonically against a degraded everyday life. Joyce's mock-heroic *Ulysses* turns in its very structure on this discrepancy.

Beckett's move from Dublin to Paris, then, was in one sense a break from nationalist Ireland to modernist, cosmopolitan Europe. Yet there was a good deal of continuity involved as well. For one thing, nationalism (a thoroughly modern phenomenon) has much in common with some currents of modernism. Both seek to move forward into the future with their eyes fixed on the past. For another thing, early twentieth-century Ireland fulfilled all three classical conditions, as Perry Anderson has defined them, for producing a modernism of its own.[2] It had an impressive lineage of high culture for artists to plunder and dismantle; it was in the throes of political revolution; and it was experiencing the impact of modernization for the first time. What emerged from all this, to be sure, was a modernist movement rather than an avant-garde – a Yeats rather than a Mayakovsky, a George Moore rather than a Piscator, the Abbey Theatre rather than the Bauhaus. In Beckett's eyes, this failed to cut deep enough.

Even so, Irish culture was hospitable to anti-realist experiment as its English counterpart was for the most part not. Realism had never been the favoured mode of Irish fiction, from the fantasy extravaganzas of the Celtic sagas to the Gothic of Maturin, Lefanu and Bram Stoker, and the great anti-novels of Sterne, Joyce and O'Brien. If Ireland was in some ways a traditionalist society, its traditions were peculiarly fractured and disrupted by a history of colonial intervention; and this meant that it was no stranger to the estranged, fragmented, unstable self, all of which played a role in the flowering of a distinctively Irish modernism. The progressive narratives of realism made little sense in such a stagnant, de-industrialised nation. Nor did realism's assured totalities. Language in Ireland had for long been a political minefield rather than a taken-for-granted reality, a fact which (as with Joyce) lent itself easily to the verbal self-consciousness of modernist art.

From Dublin to Paris, then, was not so huge a leap. It was a good deal shorter, as both Joyce and Beckett were to discover, than from Dublin to London. The cosmopolitan sympathies of both men helped to drive them out of their provincially minded, inward-looking native land; yet Ireland has also had a long tradition of looking over the heads of the British to the Continent, all the way from the peripatetic monks of the Middle Ages to the corporate executives of the Celtic Tiger. Even nationalism is a thoroughly international phenomenon, and the Irish species of it which Joyce and Beckett spurned had fruitful contacts with India, South Africa, Egypt, Afghanistan and a number of other places. It was not a matter of a simple opposition between home and abroad.

Nor is it a question of a simple coupling of Joyce and Beckett. In an illuminating discussion, Casanova shows how the two men went their different literary ways in the pursuit of similar anti-representational ends. If Beckett aimed to have no style, Joyce sought to imitate every style he could lay his hands on. If Beckett wanted to purge words of their meanings, Joyce dreamt of laying meaning on so thick that the English language would crumble to pieces in his grasp. Beckett, always an ascetic, chooses the *via negativa* of non-meaning, while his compatriot pursued the carnivalesque path of polyphony. Beckett's frugal language is among other things a reaction to the baroque hyperbole of Irish nationalist rhetoric. The celebrated avant-garde materiality of the word struck the younger Irish author as, in his own term, 'terrible'. In his search for a 'literature of the unword', language was to be eliminated, not foregrounded.

Since eliminating meaning is an impossible literary project even for a Mallarmé, writing itself becomes for Beckett the very signifier of the failure which so gripped his imagination. In a superb passage in the book, Casanova shows us how it was just this insight into the ineluctability of literary failure which enabled Beckett to find his feet as an author. He would not go the way of Yeats and Dublin, or of Shaw and London; but for a while he could not go the way of the avant-garde either, since an enormous obstacle named Joyce loomed up to block that path. In Bloomian terms, Joyce was the strong precursor to Beckett's belated ephebe – or, as they say in Ireland today, *Ulysses* is the nightmare from which Dublin is trying to awaken. Beckett will finally find a way around this daunting presence by placing the very impediment to writing at the centre of his writing, transforming the question of failure into the very form of his art, telling incessantly of the failure to tell. He will accept that though he won't write, can't write, has nothing to say and nothing with which to say it, he must write. The act of literature thus becomes a kind of empty Kantian imperative, a law without logic, an obligation without content. Like desire, it is nothing personal.

What finally strikes one most about this book is its remarkably ambitious scope. Packed into its brief compass are reflections on Irish history and European philosophy, some scrupulous analysis of individual texts, speculations on the artistic avant-garde, a fascinating excursus on Beckett and Dante, along with a coherent and provocative viewpoint on Beckett's work as a whole. One can have no doubt that the maestro himself would have admired its elegant economy.

Preface

Ill Seen Ill Read

As depicted in the fearsome, hieratic photographs imposed by official portraiture, Beckett has come to embody, at least in France, the prophetic, sacred mission assigned the writer by devotees of literature. Accordingly, he has been assimilated to a vague metaphysics, in a strange, solitary place, where suffering permits only a well-nigh inarticulate, shapeless language, a kind of pure cry of pain, cast just as it comes on to paper.

As if he alone represented a kind of poetic beyond, Beckett has only ever been read as the messenger or oracle of the truth of 'being'. *The Unnamable*, writes Maurice Blanchot, is 'a being without being, who can neither live nor die, stop or start, the empty space in which the idleness of an empty speech speaks'.[1] This representation of poetic tragedy, which is but one of the countless forms of literature's annexation by philosophers, reduces the poet to the passive, archaic function of inspired mediator, charged with 'unveiling being'. ('Ah, the old questions, the old answers, there's nothing like them'[2], says Beckett who, in irony at least, surpasses his commentators.) Even though the jargon of 'authenticity' was alien to him, the obscurity and strangeness of his texts had to be reduced to the only legitimate form of profundity. As early as the 1950s, Blanchot's view became in France the sole authorized commentary, helping to 'fabricate' a tailor-made Beckett, hero of 'pure' criticism. Lacking a history, a past, an inheritance or a project, Beckett disappeared under the flashy garb of poetic canonization.

This heroic imagery has proved one of the surest ways to obscure the specificity of literary form, to refuse Beckett any aesthetic impulse, the search for a form therewith being reduced to an artifice unworthy of the quest for 'authenticity'. Thus, apropos of *The Unnamable*, Blanchot writes of a book 'without cheating or subterfuge . . . in which aesthetic sentiments are no longer apposite'.[3] The (apparent) obscurity of Beckett's texts has served the obscurantist designs of Blanchot-style criticism.

A reconstruction of Beckett's trajectory, and of the history of his oeuvre, leads to the conclusion that such hermeneutic glaciation has not simply masked the meaning of his literary project, but inverted it. Thus he has been celebrated and consecrated in the name of an idea of poetry he always fought against. His refusal of the presuppositions underlying realism, representation, and credence in literary 'truth' can only be understood if we hypothesize that he spent his whole life working on a radical aesthetic revolution: literary abstraction. Yet it is in the name of what he called such 'outdated conventions', and above all in the name of the pathos of 'being', that he became one of the twentieth century's most famous and established writers.

Was his oeuvre so prejudicial to the very idea of poetry that it had to be dissolved in the imposing machinery for the normalization of literature?

Obliged to write after Joyce and, so as not to imitate him, beyond Joyce, Beckett embarked on the road of a different modernity at the level of form. The literary abstraction he invented, at the cost of a lifetime's enormous effort, in order to put literature on a par with all the major artistic revolutions of the twentieth century – especially pictorial abstraction – was to be based on an unprecedented literary combinatory. The art of logic was placed in the service of 'abstractivation', a dynamic peculiar to each text, which proceeds from words to the withdrawal of meaning – that is, from meaning to delivering realist representation its quietus. In order to break with signification and the referent, inherent in language, Beckett does not work on the sonorous materiality of the word. Instead, he is led to question, one after the other, all the ordinary conditions of possibility of literature – the subject, memory, imagination, narration, character, psychology, space and time, and so forth – on which, without our being aware of it, the whole historical edifice of literature rests, so as to achieve the gradual erasure of its images in 'the dim and void'.

Together with Joyce, Beckett is one of the contemporary writers who has prompted the most commentaries and analyses – something compounded in his case by the bilingualism that has entailed the construction of a dual critical tradition, in English and French.[4] Everything – or virtually everything – there is to say about him has already been said. But it suffices to switch critical standpoints, and to extend to literature the principle of 'historical inquiry' proposed by Spinoza in order to restore to sacred texts their meaning, to discover multiple traces of the formalist intention of his project – traces that have usually gone unnoticed, because they did not form part of explanation via miracles. It is therefore a question of engaging in a kind of meticulous examination – and setting out in search of minor indices that in isolation might seem insignificant and even over-interpreted, but which, when brought together, end up forming a consistent pattern. These indices illuminate the oeuvre by rendering the principles of its genesis visible. Better, they make the problems Beckett posed himself – that is, the set of literary possibilities he had to operate with in order to 'invent' his own solution – intelligible. Beckett would work for thirty years to bring literature into modernity, to develop an aesthetic answer to personal questions that are also literary investigations: those of defeat, failure, the 'worst'.

Thus, 'historical inquiry' will enable us to discover that the project governing Beckett's writing is not, as official criticism would have it, radically strange in kind – a meteorite abruptly and as if miraculously fallen from the sky, without precedents, referents or descendants. On the contrary, his greatness consists in his confrontation with the set of aesthetic issues and debates that were contemporaneous with him. Far from being frozen in the bombast consubstantial with the rhetoric of Being, Beckett more than anyone else was concerned with aesthetic modernity. From the Second World War onwards, he deliberately situated himself in relation to the whole literary and pictorial avant-garde he mixed with in Paris – and definitely not Existentialism or the Theatre of the Absurd, whose pre-suppositions were alien to him.

However, in order to advance exegesis of Beckett's intention, and understand why he made such an enormous effort to tear himself away from the commonest presuppositions of literature, we must also understand the desperate impasse he was trapped in, which he could only escape from through abstraction. In other words, it is necessary to go further back in his history and the history of his original literary space: Ireland. His project is inseparable from the itinerary, seemingly utterly contingent and external, that led him from Dublin to Paris.

From one book to the next, this search became increasingly systematic, as if Beckett gradually discovered the stylistic constraints and forms required for the coherence of his project. In the end, it would be *Worstward Ho* that radicalized, and took furthest, the formal combinatory whereby he carried out one of the greatest literary revolutions of the twentieth century.

1

Ars Combinatoria

With his first publications in French in the 1950s, critical prejudices emerged in a kind of double-blind to obstruct access to each of Beckett's texts. They have had enormous theoretical consequences.[1] Commentaries on Beckett's writing as testimony to the 'unsayable', the 'essential', and even – the height of misinterpretation the 'inarticulate' – are now too numerous to count. Refusal of the formal character of this literary undertaking, and belief in a kind of inspired passivity on the writer's part, have resulted, for example, in the emergence of a critical consensus around the notion of 'confusion'. 'Criticism,' writes Bruno Clément for example in summarizing the various hermeneutic positions on the subject, 'converges in regarding the increasing scarcity, and sometimes disappearance, of signs of formal organization (parts, chapters, paragraphs, and even sentences) as the positive mark of an essential disorder that has affected the oeuvre, thereby stripping it of any genuinely technical characteristics.'[2]

It is perhaps with *Worstward Ho*, one of Beckett's last texts, that the distance between the standard interpretation (derived from Blanchotien presuppositions), which confers on this text – as on all the others – a disorder considered inherent in the ultimate expression of existential suffering, and the interpretation imposed by a systematic analysis, becomes most apparent.

> On. Say on. Be said on. Somehow on. Till nohow on. Said nohow on. Say for be said. Missaid. From now say for be missaid.

> Say a body. Where none. No mind. Where none. That at least. A place. Where none. For the body. To be in. Move in. Out of. Back into. No. No out. No back. Only in. Stay in. On in. Still.

All of old. Nothing else ever. Ever tried. Ever failed. No matter. Try
again. Fail again. Fail better.[3]

A first reading of *Worstward Ho*, it is true, conveys the impression of a
discourse that fades out in a kind of paratactic inarticulation. Beckett had
seemingly never gone so far in the direction of hermeticism and literal
obscurity. But the power of critical bias precludes observing and understanding Beckett's project as it unfolds in this text. If we overturn the
prejudice of non-meaning and confusion associated with Beckett's writing,
we can bring out strict rules of composition and organization. *Worstward Ho*
is a summit of Beckett's *ars combinatoria*, prodigiously controlled and
devised, the magisterial conclusion to the whole oeuvre.

So we have the worst, posited in the title as a goal to be reached, as a
professed project, and which is to be understood not as an approximate,
random evocation of the oeuvre, but precisely as an algorithm, a generative
formula from which Beckett has produced the ensuing text. The title is, of
course, a parody of Charles Kingsley's well-known *Westward Ho* and,
through this migratory irony, signals both motion and direction. The worst
is what must now be striven for – the end aimed at but not yet attained.
Attesting to this is the first word of the text – 'on' – expressing continua-
tion, effort, movement, a kind of resolute 'forward'. Beckett immediately
raises the problem with a quasi-mathematical rigour: how to say the worst
and how to work incessantly to worsen the worst? If, by definition, 'said is
missaid' whatever one says, how, stylistically, can one convey the idea of
the worst and say it ever worse? How can one win the incredible wager of a
'better' that would be a successful statement of the worst? To this question
of the how, Beckett responds in the first paragraph by adopting two of the
modalities allowed by English through variations on the adverb of manner
'how': the worst will be reached by setting out from 'somehow' to arrive at
the point of 'nohow': 'On. Say on. Be said on. Somehow on. Till nohow
on. Said nohow on.'

Beckett thus states the only two modalities that he will use in the text to
attain the worst and, at the same time, defines the minimal form in which
he has *committed* himself to saying it: 'somehow' can only be said on the
basis of a syntax limited to the essential, a unique punctuation, a vocabulary
restricted and reduced to words of the worst. It is as if he was giving himself
the word and the thing at the same time – an ultimate, extreme attempt
finally to make what one says and how one says it coincide. The worst will

therefore be written in the precise gap between these two words. It will be written to the extent and for as long as one can write it, as best one can, until one can no longer do so. By immediately positing them as modes of writing, he makes 'somehow' and 'nohow' things; he substantivizes them and represents them as two points on a line, given as a beginning and an end between which the book will be written.

Later in the text, the terms in which Beckett has posed the problem become clearer: the word 'blank', which makes its first appearance on p. 31, signals the distance that still remains to be covered, in order to attain the 'nohow' which is so desired as an end (in all senses) of the text: 'Blanks for nohow on. How long? Blanks how long till somehow on? Again somehow on. All gone when nohow on. Time gone when nohow on' (p. 31). That is, at the final 'nohow', everything – or virtually everything – will have to have disappeared, including and in the first instance time: what is somehow said, as best one can, throughout the text is still of the order of the possible – that is, of the order of time. When one can still act, it is because a future, even an immediate one, can still be envisaged. The point of 'nohow', on the other hand, positing that there is nothing left to do, is not in time; it is the culmination of the worst. At this point, words too will have disappeared: 'Try better worse another stare when with words than when not. When somehow than when nohow' (pp. 38–9). In the same way, the text's verbs are mainly employed in the infinitive and past participle, without the mobility of verbal 'tenses'.

Worstward Ho is perhaps an ultimate, paradoxical, aporetic poetic art: trying everything, trying again, forging ahead as best one can, to the point where it is no longer possible, to the point of the 'nohow' that resonates like a strange victory at the very end of the text, when the programme foreshadowed in the initial equation is repeated *word for word*: 'Nohow less. Nohow worse. Nohow naught. Nohow on. Said nohow on' (p. 47).

Once these two modalities have been posited as the text's generative formula, Beckett states the first of the numerous rules that are going to punctuate *Worstward Ho*, each new rule being designated by the 'from now' that fixes the syntactical or lexical conventions as we proceed: 'Said for missaid' (p. 37). Thus henceforth, every time we encounter 'said' we should read 'missaid'. The law of 'somehow' involves the necessity of an unstable text that fixes, at the very moment it is written, its own laws of functioning. It recounts nothing but its internal genesis; and it endlessly explains how and why it needs to be written in this particular form at each instant. We remain in the extraordinary double-bind of a rule that is always provisional and shaky, open to alteration at the very moment it is stated. And the initial resolution of sticking in the gap between the two modes of 'how' is also that of sticking to a precarious position, in a permanent self-rectification, in an uncertainty that is itself only ever formulated on a provisional basis. The worst might never happen. It is not a question of retaining at any price a posture of rigour, the static imposition of a stylistic constraint, or a novel metaphysical position, but of accepting the inevitable shakiness of 'somehow', which is likewise part of the worst in that it leads to its own problematization.

Better Worse

The most formalist is not necessarily the most disembodied. It is through the practice of form that the most acute experience of tragedy finds a decisive, radical and radically new form. If 'said is missaid' en route to the worst, there is only one solution for 'worse missaid': the position of generalized pejoration.

First operation: transform all idiomatic expressions in which 'well', 'good' and the like feature to pejorate them: 'that will do just as badly', 'for bad and all', and so forth. But the change of sign only pejorates the semantic and syntactical surface of the text and, if one likes, indicates the major lines of the project, which is efficient solely in being systematic and pushing to the utmost limit the very idea of the worst that is in play. To missay is to try to say the worst: you can only missay the worst if you want to give yourself a chance to say it, to make the worst to be said and words for the worst coincide, and hence to say the worst as badly as possible. *Worstward Ho*, assembling all earlier efforts, is a mechanism of *ars combinatoria* in the mathematical sense, since it attempts, on the basis of the minimum number of elements (the least also being the basis of its definition of the bad), all the operations and combinations that can syntactically be realized. For example: 'Of all so far missaid the worse missaid. So far. Not till nohow worse missay say worse missaid' (pp. 35–6). The terminus of this line of reasoning is that it is necessary to fail to say the worst so as to remain within the order of the worst. To fail to say the worst is to provide the optimal statement of it. Becket thus supplies the rule of this novel game (and a strict interrogation of words is to be understood here): 'That little better worse. Till words for worser still. Worse words for worser still' (p. 41).

Second operation: worsen the three quasi-narrative elements or figures. Beckett states them, enumerates them, and gives them a coding so as to designate them more simply on each occasion: 'From now *one* for the kneeling one. As from now *two* for the twain . . . As from now *three* for the head' (p. 20).[4] Thus we find them distinct, numbered, identified: one, a 'bowed back'; two, a 'twain' – an old man and a child, hand in hand; three, a '[h]ead sunk on crippled hands. Clenched staring eyes' (p. 13).

Through these three figures, we see the labour of literary objectification and materialization at work. The total absence of personal pronouns throughout the text is merely a rhetorical, superficial sign of Beckett's refusal to adhere to the conventions of literary subjectivism. The emphatic presence of the 'head', by contrast, is its most refined expression: it is the materialized presence of a 'worsened' subject, which, by means of this unprecedented provocation, has become a mere object. The 'head' and its 'some soft of mind' are not representations of a metaphysical subject, but mere objective images that themselves produce images. 'Say a body. Where none. No mind,' Beckett had posited as a preliminary, in the opening lines of his text (p. 7).

To these three figures we must add a semblance of scenery: the dim and the void. To the question 'Where now?' with which *The Unnamable* opens, Beckett now answers, as if modelling himself on the mysterious 'backgrounds' of Manet's paintings, by asserting an empty, dark background against which his images stand out. Therewith he has found, it seems, the precise equivalent of the 'thing' painted (according to him) by Bram Van Velde: 'The immobile thing in the void – here at last is the visible thing, the pure object. I see no other.'[5] The dim and the void are Beckett's response to the spatial conventions posited by the whole literary tradition as conditions of possibility of literature. These five elements are on course for the worst, between 'somehow' and 'nohow'.

Since the book is written in a striving for the 'worse than worst', each formulation of its five worsenable objects is going to be repeatedly taken up, imperceptibly altered, broken down with rules stated in conformity with the coherence of the text, towards that melting into the night where the dim itself would disappear. Without unfolding the whole process of 'worsening' of the five figures here, let us take the example of 'two' – the twain – in its gradual metamorphoses. It makes its appearance on p. 12: 'In the dim void bit by bit an old man and child . . . Hand in hand with equal plod they go . . . Slowly with never a pause plod on and never recede.

Backs turned. Both bowed.' They reappear on p. 16: 'Dim hair. Dim white and hair so fair that in the dim light dim white. Black greatcoats to heels. Dim black. Bootheels. Now the two right. Now the two left.'

We have hitherto been in the register of the 'bad'. On p. 21 an initial comparative break is made. By a strict grammatical progression, we pass from 'bad' to 'worse': 'A pox on bad. Mere bad. Way for worse. Pending worse still. First worse.' It is now a question of 'failing better' by passing 'from bad to worsen'. And to this end Beckett provides a decisive new rule for his definition of the worst: 'Add? Never' (p. 21). Accordingly, he is now going to embark on a labour of subtraction and diminution: 'The boots. Better worse bootless. Bare heels. Now the two right. Now the two left . . . Barefoot unreceding on. Better worse so' (p. 23).

With 'back', Beckett indicates seven pages later that he is returning to 'two': 'That said on back to try worse say the plodding twain . . . Least worst failed of all the worse failed shades . . . And yet say first the worst perhaps worst of all the old man and child. Worst in need of worse' (pp. 30–31). This is another new step, because the comparative 'worse' is abandoned for the superlatives 'worst' and 'the worst'. In passing, Beckett 'unsays', as he does several times, an initial affirmation that proves false from the standpoint of the text's logic: 'Here now held holding. As when first said. Ununsaid when worse said. Away. Held holding hands!' (p. 32). Inverting the process ('Ununsaid when worse said'), with the critical irony that accompanies each of his technical feats Beckett restores, in a double negative that renders it positive, the first formulation, which turns out to be best from the standpoint of the logic of the worst.

Having next stressed not the worst but the least ('So leastward on . . . To last unlessenable least how loath to leasten' [p. 33]), he undoes the twain but not conclusively, so as to retain a new possibility of worsening it: 'Gone held holding hands they plod apart . . . Not worsen yet the rift. Save for some after nohow somehow worser on' (p. 34). And then he increases the void between the old man and the child: 'Two once so one. From now rift a vast. Vast of void atween . . . That little better worse' (p. 41). In the final references to the twain, the three shadows merge, indistinct and alike: all three have become '[t]opless baseless hind-trunks. Legless plodding on' (p. 43).

James Knowlson has highlighted the fact that images of childhood recur in Beckett's texts, including the most obscure and abstract of them.[6] The image of an old man and a child hand in hand, present in numerous texts in various forms, is one of those figures that Beckett has called 'obsessional'. And we cannot resist seeing in it the moving, evanescent sketch of a final image of his father, a memory of childhood happiness, a trace in the memory of the old man that he has himself become. Through these polished forms Beckett also summons up what is most intimate and most hidden. The seemingly most mechanical variations of the 'twain' are also the most pathetic: 'Two once so one. From now rift a vast. Vast of void atween' is an evocation, in an incredible résumé, of the past closeness of father and child and the irreparable death of the father that has separated them, when the rending apart of their previously clasped hands has become irreversible. We also discover at the end that the upright body, and then bowed shadow (the worsened body), unidentifiable, is the pathetic one of a woman: 'Nothing and yet a woman. Old and yet old. On unseen knees. Stooped as loving memory some old gravestones stoop. In that old graveyard. Names gone and when to when. Stoop mute over the graves of none' (p. 45).

Worstward Ho is also a virtually explicit synthesis of Beckett's formal questions and uncertainties. In it he explains his previous attempts, the solutions hit on in other books – in connection with the disposition of the body, for example: 'No choice but stand . . . Somehow stand . . . Simply up. A time when try how. Try see. Try say. How first it lay. Then somehow knelt. Bit by bit . . . Till up at last. Not now. Fail better worse now' (p. 10). The same decision in favour of symmetrical austerity is made as regards place: 'A place. Where none. A time when try see. Try say. How small. How vast. How if not boundless bounded. Whence the dim. Not now. Know better now. Unknow better now' (p. 11). Here Beckett relates how he tried in other texts to refer to something out of frame, a reality existing outside textual closure. But in *Worstward Ho* there are no longer any concessions to the ultimate conventions of literary realism, no longer things or places (there are still some objects at the beginning of the text – boots and overcoat – but they very rapidly disappear). Beckett accomplishes his project of an absolutely self-sufficient writing, generating its own syntax, vocabulary, self-ordained grammar, even creating terms that respond exclusively to the logic of the pure space of the text: no more referents, no more attempts to imitate reality or provide an equivalent to it, no more direct links of transposition or description of the world – a text that is indebted solely to itself for the fact that it could be written.

A Poetic Art

The logic of the worst implies crossing, entangling, piling up all the comparatives in degressive order (strict, precise worsening is carried out with the comparatives of 'bad' for the three shadows and with those of 'less' for the dim and the void). In this respect, the prepositional economy of English allows for infinite construction and alliterative play that yield the most dishevelled forms and proliferating constructions –'best bad worse of all', 'for want of worser worst', 'unworseable worst', 'unworsenable worst', 'worse better later', 'unmoreable unlessable unworseable evermost almost void' – and the recurrent form of the whole text, emblem of this oxymoronic universe: 'How better worse so-missay?'.

These comparatives, which all strive for the inverted perfection of the aesthetic of lessness, yoked to this implacable logic, are suddenly confronted with the rule already stated above: 'Add? Never' (p. 21). In the land of the worst, logically enough, one can only subtract, diminish. It is then no longer possible to integrate the little word 'more' into a formulation that is admissible in terms of the rule of the worst. But what if 'more' means 'less', as in 'more obscure' for example? Beckett raises the question, advances, circumvents grammatical obstacles and difficulties, and then states the law: 'Back unsay better worse by no stretch more. If more dim less light then better worse more dim. Unsaid then better worse by no stretch more. Better worse may no less than less be more' (p. 37). As we can see, such a project involves an impeccable logic and coherence. And that is why Beckett, on the basis of his rules, never stops raising and circumventing all the contradictions, paradoxes and impossibilities generated by pejoration and failure. To state the bad as badly as possible in order to try extricate oneself from it, and make obsessive images of the worst disappear, is not unproblematic.

As has been said, the text operates by 'backs' in order to worsen some particular formulation. Reflexivity and examination of the systematicity of the mechanism occupy a very great deal of space. The writing progresses to the beat of an astonishing play of questions and answers, of interrogation of the consistency of the text and the validity and effectiveness of the process. We might even imagine that it involves a kind of dialogue, a text with two voices, with questions and objections from an alter ego who is rather sick and tired, rather doubtful, and who chalks up all the errors and inconsistencies: 'What? Yes'; 'No mind and pain? Say yes' (pp. 8–9).

Among the logical objections that arise straightaway are those of place and time. These two founding instances of any literary narrative, referring at once to the text's field and what is out of frame, are subject to constant alterations that emerge like second thoughts whenever it is necessary to make concessions to grammatical and referential order. One cannot advance the hypothesis of an absolute independence of the text with respect to the world, grammar and literary convention. One can simply propose, because one wishes to aim for it, the 'minimal minimum' before the disappearance of words and meaning. As early as p. 11, the description of place is problematic: 'A place. Where none . . . Know only no out of. No knowing how know only no out of. Into only. Hence another. Another place where none. Whither once no return. No. No place but the one . . . Whence never once in . . . Beyond less. Thence less there' (pp. 11–12). Formulating the objection to himself (to enter one place it is necessary to leave another and envisage positing at least two places, including something out of frame, not in question in our constraints), Beckett explains the rule, which is essential, of his project's independence (no beyond or beneath, no transcendence or reference to the world). Time, defined at the outset as '[a]ll of old. Nothing else ever' (p. 7), raises precisely the same deductive problem of a time transcending the pastless present of writing: 'No once. No once in the pastless now. No not none. When before worse the shades? The dim before more? When if not once?' (p. 38).

'From now', 'so far', 'later', 'now' only explain and articulate the internal time of the text, the chronological unfolding of its formation, its autonomous conditions of possibility. In contrast, the 'least minimal minimum' known of time, of place, of elements to worsen, necessarily implies something beyond the text that Beckett seeks to diminish solely so as to proceed in the direction of the worst. It is the irreducible residue of a referent, even when completely disembodied, even when reduced to its logical structure (the void, for example), which Beckett tries to get round by 'somehow'. Thus, from defeats to concessions the way of 'better missaying' is imperceptibly altered. For example, examination of 'least' leads to a semi-defeat, resignation to an irreducible minimum that will henceforth have to be integrated into the rules: 'Least never to be naught. Never to naught be brought. Never by naught be nulled. Unnullable least. Say that best worst. With leastening words say least best worse. For want of worser worst. Unlessenable least best worst' (p. 32). It is this irreducible residue that Beckett desperately tries to circumvent, sidestep, coax into arriving at all costs at 'nohow'.

But there are some residues before which one must resolve to surrender: these are the three elements that resist both worsening and disappearing (and the progression of the text is also the disclosure of a strange power-lessness in the face of them).

The void first of all. The law of its immutability is stated very early on: 'The void. Unchanging. Say now unchanging . . . The void. How try say? How try fail? No try no fail' (p. 17). But he makes a few attempts: 'That narrow field. Know no more. See no more. Say no more. That alone. That little much of void alone' (p. 18); 'Unworsenable void. Never less. Never more. Never since first said never unsaid never worse said' (p. 42). Only to conclude in irritation at the end of the text: 'A pox on void. Unmoreable unlessable unworseable evermost almost void' (pp. 42–3).

Next, the dim. Beckett tries to worsen it in the sense of darkness, but it resists any metamorphosis. It gives rise to some virtuoso comparative variations that nevertheless fail: 'Dim undimmed. Or dimmed to dimmer still. To dimmost dim. Leastmost in dimmost dim. Utmost dim. Leastmost in utmost dim. Unworsenable worst' (p. 33).

Finally, the head, aporia of aporias, observed and observing, 'scene and seer of all' (p. 23). The head is the only element in the text that must necessarily, desperately be both within and without, in the text and outside it: the head that says, that sees, that forms images, sees its head in its head and very rapidly – paradox of infinite inter-locking – is confronted with the impossibility of making itself disappear without erasing the text along with it. Of the three 'shades', the head is the one that Beckett most tortures, disfigures, scars, gradually reducing it to its most salient features ('stares' for the eyes). It is the very mark of the text's reflection on itself and its conditions of possibility. Reduplication under-scores the logical contradiction. The first formulation of it is to be found on p. 10: 'Head sunk on crippled hands. Vertex vertical. Eyes clenched. Seat of all. Germ of all.' The setting and ordering imply that the head is at once a shadow on the stage and an element on course for the worst: a spectator ('clenched staring eyes' [p. 13]) before which stand the twain, the bowed one, the void, and the dim ('same narrow void. Before the staring eyes' [p. 19]); and, finally, matrix of all that (and of itself). The head is the begetter begotten: 'On back better worse to fail the head said seat of all. Germ of all. All? If of all of it too. Where if not there it too?

There in the sunken head the sunken head' (pp. 18–19). This is proof that Beckett pushes the coherence of his project to the point of raising in his text the issue of his own presence-absence; he incorporates into his 'setting' the hand that writes and the head that thinks, supplying a kind of self-portrait in action. It is a disenchanted, prosaic self-portrait of the writer refusing the presuppositions of consciousness to the extent that he objectifies himself as manufacturing images in his own images – that is, by placing himself in the painting, like Velázquez representing himself painting in the background of *Las Meninas*. He is the painter and the subject of the painting, represented and representing, 'scene and seer of all'. In connection with the 'centre' of this painting, at the beginning of *The Order of Things* Michel Foucault enumerates what he calls the 'three "observing" functions' that we find in *Worstward Ho*: 'In it [the centre] there occurs an exact superimposition of the model's gaze as it is being painted, of the spectator's as he contemplates the painting, and of the painter's as he is composing the picture'. 'The entire picture,' Foucault writes, 'is looking out at a scene for which it is itself the scene.'[7]

As a result, in the game of the worst 'that head in that head' is going to be devalued into a 'sunken skull' (p. 22); the 'clenched staring eyes' will lose their eyelids; and the 'remains of mind' (p. 29) gradually disintegrate into 'some soft of mind' which 'oozes' (p. 33). As in the Vanities metaphorically representing death in the privileged form of a skull, Beckett worsens the head to the point of making it a single black hole: 'One dim black hole mid-foreskull. Into the hell of all. Out of the hell of all' (p. 44). This is the 'what little left' (p. 46) that makes it possible to conclude and reach the point where one can no longer advance ('nohow'); the residue of mind that remains for saying that one has come as close as possible to the dissolution of meaning, but that in still saying it – even to the minimum extent possible – one is not quite there yet. On several occasions in the text we find an interrogation, logical and insoluble in the objectivist system set in place by Beckett, of the origin of words: 'Whose words? Ask in vain' (p. 19); and later: 'Worsening words whose unknown . . . Now for to say as worst they may only they only they . . . Nothing save what they say' (p. 29). Alternatively put, the task laid down in the first paragraph of acceding to the worst from 'somehow' to 'nohow' is also that of proceeding from words to their disappearance via the gradual withdrawal of meaning. In the order of lessness – that is, the 'nearly unseen' and the 'nearly unsaid' – what words say cannot be completely eliminated; it is impossible not to know anything ('[t]oo much to hope' [p. 9]), but it is possible to know '[e]nough to know no knowing' (p. 30).

Worstward Ho originates in an utterly coherent aesthetic programme, which at the outset posits its end (term) as its end (goal): what counts at the end, in the endgame, is not the disappearance, the final failure of the text, but instead a project that determines its end once the rule, the algorithm, has exhausted all its possibilities. The last words, repeated from the programme clearly announced at the beginning ('Said nohow on') resonate like a cry of victory: the success of the worst of failures.

The equation[8] stated and solved by *Worstward Ho* therefore provides (strict) irrefutable proof of a formidable formal ambition, without precedent in the history of literature, of a logical, combinatory option in the service of a new literary form. *Worstward Ho* is not the evocation of a nihilistic stance or the representation of ontological tragedy, but a kind of ultimate poetic art: Beckett delivers his theory of literary abstraction in practice and elaborates an abstract text at the very point when he explains how he writes it.

It is possibly also a literary testament of sorts, discreet, disclaimed, tacit: the assertion of an aesthetic revolution with which Beckett has never been credited.

But it would be too easy to reduce his set of discoveries to a pure formalism: the search for the appropriate road to abstract art in literature led him not only to alter the forms of organization of the text, but to undermine the foundations of literature. His mere problematization of the subject, of psychological interiority, or of the imagination disclosed, possibly for the first time in the history of forms (at all events, with such demonstrative power), that literature rests entirely on the presuppositions of the philosophy of the subject. By means of a simple displacement, Beckett denounces the taken-for-granted realist assumptions on which the whole literary edifice is based.

With *Worstward Ho* Beckett created a pure object of language, which is totally autonomous since it refers to nothing but itself. As if it was working towards a black hole from which there could issue no trace of representation, no form that might recall, even vaguely, a body . . . Without a subject, without scenery, standing out on a black (dim), empty background, freed from any temporal or spatial reference-points, the images of *Worstward Ho* inaugurate abstract literature: they are headed towards a working drawing of abstraction or darkness.

2

Youth and Genesis

This kind of precise reading nevertheless reduces textual analysis to unravelling a enigma exclusively on the basis of the materials provided, as in detective novels, by the text itself. It seems to vindicate partisans of a pure reading of pure texts who want to believe – like Roman Jakobson analysing Baudelaire's 'Les Chats' – in their interpretative self-sufficiency. As ordinarily practised, internal reading makes it possible to understand the *how* of a literary text – that is, to dismantle its internal mechanics. But it never poses the question of its very existence (of why it exists rather than nothing); the question of *why* it exists in this particular form. It thus prevents itself from understanding the ruptures the text originates in, the terms of the implicit debate it is involved in – in short, its specific history. It postulates the a-historical character and inevitability of any text: literature is supposedly like a miracle before which we must bow down and in silence.

We can therefore opt not to stop at a description of the text, but go on to raise the necessarily historical question of 'why'. 'Historical inquiry' is then applied to the oeuvre and the literary configuration that made it possible. It returns to the conditions of its emergence, its genesis. Internal reading is unquestionably much more legitimate when applied to Beckett's late texts than any other type of text, since they are the most radically autonomous – that is, those to which, on account of Beckett's novel project, the theory of the autonomy of literature and critical discourse might exceptionally be applied. Even so, in order to understand the formal and aesthetic questions that Beckett posed himself, the way he sought to resolve them, and in order to grasp the stakes and very 'purity' of his literary project, its progressive detachment from any external determination, we must retread the path of his attainment of formal, stylistic freedom. And this path is historical.

Contrary to what is asserted by criticism inspired by Blanchot, which has severed him from his history in its entirety, Beckett belonged in the first instance, at least prior to his exile and break (which are likewise the product of his Dublin itinerary), to the Irish literary universe. His oeuvre, it is true, became increasingly autonomous, discovered and asserted its own logic, and broke its direct dependence on the original literary space. But we can only understand the set of decisive choices he made, the process of his aesthetic investigations, on the basis of his position in his original universe. The indices of a paradoxical 'Irishness', accepted and asserted by Beckett, are numerous, at least from his definitive settling in Paris – starting with his professed adherence to the Irish philosopher Berkeley's idealism; and the signs of a perfect knowledge of the specific problems bound up with the Irish literary and political universe provide a gauge of his membership of it, albeit ambivalent and denied.

Much evidence reveals him very hesitant about the idea of being assimilated, as a result of French ignorance, to the zone of English influence. Robert Pinget recounts that with a view to improving his English he had asked Beckett in writing for some addresses in England and had received an immediate reply to the effect 'that he had no addresses in England but several in Ireland'.[1] John Fletcher recalls that Beckett always travelled with a passport issued by the Republic of Ireland.[2] And E. M. Cioran, naturally without relating the literary tastes of Beckett, who had a passion for the writings of his compatriot Swift, to a national history, but attributing them to an unexplained affinity between their oeuvres, recounts:

> I do not know how we arrived at Swift, even though, on reflection, there was nothing anomalous about the transition, given the lugubrious character of his raillery. Beckett told me that he was reading *Gulliver's Travels* and that his favourite part was the 'country of the Houyhnhnms', especially the scene where Gulliver is wild with fright and disgust at the approach of a female Yahoo.[3]

But even the recent criticism that seeks to adopt an 'external standpoint' on Beckett's work only ventures to accord Ireland a place on the basis of the category of the 'imaginary'. Bruno Clément, who has nevertheless renewed interpretation of the texts by studying rhetoric in Beckett, asserts for example that the Ireland 'which haunts Beckett's oeuvre [is an] imaginary

Ireland . . . Beckett's Ireland is therefore strictly speaking neither Ireland (since it is imaginary), nor Beckettian (since its function in the work is more important than its character), because it is above all a memory.'[4] The primacy of the 'imaginary' over the real, posited as preliminary to any literary commentary, disembodies and by the same token derealizes any literary enterprise. Why should Beckett's Ireland be imaginary *a priori*? Why must a literary project be uprooted from the everyday world to render it worthy of the most noble idea of literature?

'Home Olga'

The early writings make it possible to understand everything that the literary work of maturity would gradually efface or blur: the aesthetic breaks, clashes, rejections and positions; the admirations and filiations. Here I therefore propose to follow Beckett's oeuvre as it unfolds, not so as to discover in it the anticipation of the writing to come, but in order to reconstruct the conditions of its emergence step by step. And I propose to do this without falling into the trap of the 'retrospective illusion', constitutive of run-of-the-mill literary criticism, which employs the early texts only in order to validate *a posteriori* its most widespread interpretations; and which 'finds', once the oeuvre has been completed, a proof of its genius in its very unity, while forgetting that unity (like totality) is only an effect retrospectively reconstructed by criticism itself. Since it frequently ignores the oeuvre as history, criticism assumes that the author knows and understands that which is the very object of his investigation; what he will gradually discover through long, hard work that would have been superfluous had he known at the outset what he knows at the end, when his oeuvre is finished.

I am not referring here to commonplace recourse to biography: the specific history of literature is written in a literary mode, even (and especially) when it seems to shy away from history. It is therefore in the texts that we can try to rediscover and retrace Beckett's trajectory. Thus, the poem 'Home Olga', a 1932 acrostic dedicated to Joyce for 'Bloomsday' is, in a literary form that evokes without disclosing anything, a kind of implicit developer (in the photographic sense) of Beckett's attachment to the Irish literary space and the place he occupied in it. In sophisticated fashion, through the most cultured allusions and references, it sketches the literary Ireland of the 1930s as it appeared to Beckett.

Home Olga

J might be made sit up for a jade of hope (and exile don't you know)
And Jesus and Jesuits juggernauted in the haemorrhoidal isle,
Modo et forma anal maiden, giggling to death in stomacho.
E for the erythrite of love and silence and the sweet noo style,
Swoops and loops of love and silence in the eye of the sun and view
                                                            of the mew,

Juvante Jah and a Jain or two and the tip of a friendly yiddophile.
O for an opal of faith and cunning winking adieu, adieu, adieu;
Yesterday shall be tomorrow, riddle me that my rapparee;
Che sarà sarà che fu, there's more than Homer knows how to spew,
Exempli gratia: ecce himself and the pickthank agnus –
                                                            e.o.o.e.[5]

An aesthetic object constructed out of the letters of Joyce's name, these ten
lines simultaneously evoke the trajectory of Joyce, the stifling atmosphere
of Ireland in the 1930s and, above all, Beckett's aesthetic fascination with
someone who opted to conduct his artistic revolution in exile. 'Home
Olga' in itself encapsulates Beckett's relations with Joyce in all their
complexity – his intimacy and estrangement, his distance and humility,
his reverence and desire for independence. As a hesitant, fascinated disciple,
he demonstrates his stylistic virtuosity and simultaneously proclaims his
indebtedness and his freedom. The form, the themes, the vocabulary and
the lofty hermeticism indicate that he wishes to be understood by only one
person. The very choice of title attests to an assumed complicity. According
to Beckett himself, 'Home Olga' was a private joke in Irish circles in Paris
in the 1930s.[6] During a Dublin soirée, a bored husband had whispered to
his wife 'Home Olga!' (or 'Let's be off, Olga!') and had dragged her away
without giving her time to say goodbye to the guests. Thereafter, in similar
circumstances, the phrase had become the signal for meeting in a café
selected in advance. At the moment he swears allegiance to Joyce, Beckett
proclaims his freedom and, even in this disavowed form, the fact that he is
distancing himself.

The very structure of the poem is a knowing, erudite homage to Joyce's
work, which only an intimate knowledge of the oeuvre could authorize. It
is constructed on the three declared 'arms' of Joyce, the three cardinal

virtues stated as prolegomena to any future oeuvre in *A Portrait of the Artist as a Young Man* – 'silence, exile and cunning': 'I will try to express myself in some mode of life or art as freely as I can and as wholly as I can, using for my defense the only arms I allow myself to use – silence, exile and cunning'.[7] These are themselves associated with the three theological virtues – hope, love, faith – and with the colours that traditionally accompany them – green, red and white – metaphorically designated by a coloured stone (jade for green, erythrite for red, opal for white), and which regularly structure the poem every four lines.

This appropriation of the three founding theological virtues of Catholic morality for literary purposes – an appropriation that will be met with again in *More Pricks than Kicks*, in the even more provocative form of the 'Bovril' neon sign in Dublin: 'The lemon of faith jaundiced . . . was in a fungus of hopeless green reduced to shingles and abolished'[8] – is also an expression of disgust and hatred: exile posited as an equivalent of hope, and cunning as an equivalent of faith, leave no room for doubt about attachment to a country characterized as a 'haemorrhoidal isle'. The poem is a kind of provocative manifesto, of violent protest against the Irish religious, political and poetic order. The learned dose of pedantry and scatology, imitating Joyce, is a veritable attack on the sense of decency in 1930s Dublin, where Catholics, now in power, were to impose various forms of literary and political censorship.

We shall find in all of the young Beckett's texts this colour symbolism, which plays on the polysemy, ambiguity and arbitrariness of these mandatory, fixed equivalences. In a different register, green is the national colour of Ireland; and it was so well established as an official metaphor for the country that its symbolism had become a commonplace. Joyce himself, in his various talks, readily used the set expression 'Emerald Isle';[9] and in his memoirs Sean O'Casey recalls that at the time of independence in 1921, 'Erin was becoming the green isle in fact as in figment'.[10] Thus, in one of his first texts, playing on the same symbolism to denounce nationalist clichés, Beckett wrote:

> Isn't there enough green in this merdific island? I get on to your accursed bolide at the risk of my life at College Green . . . If it's not the Steven's Green it's Green's bloody library. 'What we want' he screamed from the sidewalk 'in this pestiferous country is red for a change and plenty of it.'[11]

The insistent scatology, in contravention of literary good taste and propriety, is another way of proclaiming Irish sterility ('Modo et forma anal maiden'),[12] bound up both with the Catholic church and with what he considered to be Dublin provincialism. To his denunciation of bigotry and insular confinement, Beckett therefore adds professed disrespect for the motherland, which was then at the centre of all intellectual and literary debates in Dublin; as well as explicit mockery of Celtic poets ('there's more than Homer knows how to spew'), followers of Yeats, who were very powerful in Dublin literary circles and claimed to be taking up the Homeric torch.

Accordingly, 'Home Olga' is not only the fascinated homage of a respectful follower, but also the violent adoption of a position, a declaration of war, a profession of faith by a young poet who has chosen his side – more aesthetic than political: a literary manifesto or, rather, a programme of aesthetic resistance to the official national poetry.

Literary Topology: Dublin, London, Paris

Fully to understand what was at stake, mention must be made of the Irish literature published around 1890 and the complex of national literary debates. Observing Beckett's itinerary, we cannot but be struck by the importance attached to three 'capital' cities – Dublin, London and Paris – which he moved between, following the obligatory itinerary of every Irish writer from the 1930s to the present. Irish literature was constituted in accordance with this triangle, not so much geographical as aesthetic, which had been invented, constructed and also closed by the generation that preceded Beckett. Yeats in Dublin had founded the original national literary position; Shaw in London occupied the canonical position of the Irishman converted to English exigencies; and Joyce refused this alternative and succeeded in reconciling the opposites by constructing Paris as a new stronghold for the Irish, excluding both the demands of national poetry and submission to English literary norms. This outline of the literary structure defined by three cities summarizes the whole specific history of Irish literature, as it was 'invented' between 1890 and 1930; and it offered any aspiring Irish writer a range of aesthetic possibilities, commitments, positions and options. Beckett's movements between these three cities were so many literary trajectories and aesthetic endeavours to find his place in a space that was at once national and international, literary and political.

Dublin: Against the 'Bardolaters'

In Dublin one of the most remarkable of Beckett's explicit public stands was no doubt his polemic against Irish 'bards'. 'Recent Irish Poetry' is one of his first texts, published in London in 1934 in the journal *Bookman*.[13] He signed it with a pseudonym not only because he published a short story in the same issue ('A Case in a Thousand'), but above all because he feared anger in Dublin following his demolition of the local and international glories of Ireland. In it he proclaimed his literary positions loud and clear by stating his refusal to follow the path of his Yeatsian elders.

'Recent Irish Poetry' aimed to establish a quasi-exhaustive panorama of the Irish poetry of the time. The attack is sharp and precise: Beckett unambiguously identified his literary opponents, whom he knew so well that he made do with quotations or even allusions to refer to them. The main enemy was 'bardolatry' – not that devotion to Shakespeare denounced by G. B. Shaw, but the whole national tradition born with Yeats and continued by Catholic intellectuals, which was still largely dominant at the beginning of the 1930s, to the extent that Beckett could write: 'contemporary Irish poets may be divided into antiquarians and others, the former in the majority, the latter kindly noticed by Mr W. B. Yeats as "the fish that lie gasping on the shore"'.[14] The 'antiquarians' were 'thermolaters – and they pullulate in Ireland – adoring the stuff of song as incorruptible, uninjurable and unchangeable'.[15] Beckett's deliberately provocative position thus went against the grain of the dominant poetic output. On several occasions he directly or indirectly targeted the greatest of the Irish 'bards' – Yeats, who was 69, Nobel Prize winner for Literature ten years earlier, famous and celebrated the world over, everywhere honoured as the greatest living poet in the English language, national hero and undisputed international celebrity.

The Irish Literary Revival in effect 'invented' the Irish tradition between 1890 and 1930.[16] Revisiting the romantic legacy that had assigned writers the task of exhuming the popular and national inheritance, and constituting literature as an expression of the 'popular soul', a group of intellectuals, the majority of them Anglo-Irish – W. B. Yeats, Lady Gregory, George Russell (AE), Edward Martyn, George Moore and others – engaged in 'fabricating' a national literature on the basis of oral practices. They collected, transcribed, translated and rewrote Celtic stories and legends. They converted popular tales into literature through poetry or drama, ennobling them; and elevated the great characters of Irish legend cycles, such as Cuchulain, to the mythical rank of embodiment of the people. Yeats gradually became the central figure in Irish national poetry. It was through his inaugural literary gesture that Ireland could lay claim to its own literary existence. By the same token, and at the same time, a generation of writers identified with Dublin and made it into a new literary capital, rivalling London.

But the poetic revival was not a purely literary movement. It was bound up with political nationalism, which it supplied with tools of emancipation. In these founding years the Irish literary question was inseparable from the national question. Ireland only became independent in 1921. Following the major national uprising of Easter 1916, which was influenced by the heroic themes of the poets of the Revival and repressed with great violence, England conceded and imposed a partition of Ireland after eight centuries of colonization and political and economic enslavement of the island: in the south, the Irish Free State; in the north, Ulster. One of Beckett's biographers, Deirdre Bair, reports that Beckett (born in 1906) still remembered 60 years later, with (he told her) 'horrified fear', the 1916 Easter Rising and fires in Dublin, which he had observed from a hilltop.

To ridicule the poetry of the Celtic legends, as did Beckett in 'Recent Irish Poetry', under the pretext of providing a panorama of contemporary Irish poetry, was therefore a heretical position in the nationalist, Celtifying Dublin of the 1920s and 30s. In the strange, precious style of a learned student characteristic of his texts of the time, he mocked the mandatory, repetitive mythical thematic of Celtic folklore with the help of periphrases and circumlocutions. For Yeats, remarked Beckett ironically, poetry possessed 'an iridescence of themes – Oisin, Cuchulain, Maeve, Tir-nanog, the Táin Bo Cuailgne, Yoga, the Crone of Beare . . . There are the specialists, but no monopolies, each poet being left perfect liberty to make his selection . . . [A] large dose of freedom may enter into the montage of these components'.[17] According to Beckett, this struggle between the academicians and the moderns was not peculiar to Ireland, but was especially intense there, 'thanks to the technique of our leading twilighters'. Here too we have an explicit allusion, at least for the Irish, to one of Yeats's most famous texts, *The Celtic Twilight*. The most noble Irish pantheon in its entirety is designated after him: James Stephens, Colum, George Russell, Austin Clarke, and Higgins, who for his part belongs to the group of 'younger antiquarians' – a way of emphasizing that what is involved is not a mere generational quarrel and some banal resumption of the battle of the Ancients and the Moderns.

The Moderns, among whom Beckett resolutely classes himself, are defined at the beginning of the text as those who have become aware of the novel situation constituted by 'the breakdown of the object': 'The artist who is aware of this may state the space that intervenes between him and the world of objects; he may state it as no-man's-land, Hellespont or vacuum, according as he happens to be feeling resentful, nostalgic or merely depressed.'[18] This definition of poetic modernity is the first tangible sign of Beckett's reflection on his own practice and the rationale for his aesthetic options. Naturally, we shall find echoes of it in his famous formula in 'Dante . . . Bruno. Vico . . . Joyce': 'here form is content, content is form' – a literary credo that would inspire his first poetic and novelistic experiments.[19] But we must also regard it as the conviction, strengthened by frequenting Joyce, of the pre-eminence of language over the world, or rather of the invariable failure of words and things to coincide. At all events, we can see why he could not adhere to any of the Celtic poetic ideologies, which tend to constitute the poet as prophet – someone who claims to speak the world and give it meaning; and we can better appreciate why his initial writings are informed by irony and self-ridicule.

It was also during this period, in the course of a stay in Dublin, that he came out against the Irish government in a short article on censorship in Ireland (which ultimately did not appear in *Transition*).[20] Beckett protested against the decree of 16 July 1929 setting up a commission charged with identifying the books authorized to circulate in the Irish Republic in accordance with moralistic criteria.

On the other hand, Beckett took an interest in Dublin's theatre life. The Abbey Theatre became one of the rallying points for all Irish intellectuals and still played a key role in national cultural life in the 1930s. All avant-garde European theatre was presented in the Irish capital at the time: Ibsen was first staged in 1913 and Beckett was present at the Gate for some productions of Pirandello. Literary modernity penetrated Dublin via innovation in drama, much more than through the novel or poetry. This was also the era of the triumph of Irish theatre. In particular, Beckett saw major plays by Synge and during his studies at Trinity College attended O'Casey's first pieces – these unquestionably being the two Irish dramatists for whom he had the greatest admiration at the time. O'Casey, from a Protestant background but a very poor family, was closer to Irish Catholics than to the Protestant bourgeoisie. Autodidact, active trade-unionist, founder-member of the Irish Citizen Army in 1914, he resigned from it the same year, took part in the 1916 Easter Rising, but withdrew fairly quickly in order to write plays that would celebrate nationalism while demonstrating the ambiguity and danger of heroic national mythologies.

In the December 1934 issue of the journal *Bookman*, Beckett published his only laudatory article, entitled 'The Essential and the Incidental' and devoted to O'Casey's *Windfalls*. Beckett deemed this collection of short stories and poems inferior to his farces: 'Mr O'Casey is a master of knockabout in this very serious and honourable sense – that he discerns the principle of disintegration in even the most complacent solidities, and activates it in their explosion.'[21] From the whole spectrum of Irish dramatic authors, Beckett thus selected the most marginal, the most improbable, the most 'dissident' figure with respect to Irish national tradition – a writer rejected by the Irish public in the name of respect for national propriety and mythology. *The Plough and the Stars*, staged in February 1926, created a scandal; the performance turned into a riot and O'Casey had to exile himself to England. For Beckett his masterpiece to this day was *Juno and the Paycock*, because that play 'communicates most fully this dramatic dehiscence, mind and world come asunder in irreparable dissociation'.[22] Beckett's admiration for O'Casey's tragic farces might be a cause for surprise today, given the militant character of pieces devoted to the description and political denunciation of the misery of the Irish people. But it was precisely the distance between subject and discourse, and hence its scepticism, that constituted all the value of this oeuvre for Beckett. O'Casey was doubtless one of the literary escape-routes that he would remember when returning to Paris, in order to elude the stylistic sway of Joyce. It was by reviving an Irish tradition that he seemed to have rejected more decisively than anyone else that Beckett suddenly became famous in Paris in 1953. And *Waiting for Godot* might also be a tragic farce that has been emptied of political charge.

An Irishman in London

Beckett therefore rejected the Ossianic ideology and aesthetic, but did not thereby adhere to the English model. Recognition from the early twentieth century of a new English-language literature in Ireland – particular by London critics – did not preclude its dependence (historical, political and literary) on London. This dependence confronted writers with a difficult choice: either to participate in the development of this new national literature in aesthetic terms dictated by the Irish debate; or to be assimilated to English literary norms and pursue the path of the imitation denounced by Joyce at the beginning of *Ulysses*, when he identifies 'the cracked lookingglass of a servant' as a symbol of Irish art.[23] For those who refused the poetic and dramatic initiatives of Dublin, London in these years still represented a literary alternative.

In order to escape the confinement and weight of Ireland – and the word 'juggernaut' employed in 'Home Olga' resonates strongly – Beckett, following the almost canonical Irish itinerary, in the first instance therefore sought exile in London. During his stay in the English capital (1934–5), he tried to start a career as a writer and critic. But he regarded all London's inhabitants as a collectively hostile mass whom it was advisable to encounter as rarely as possible; and when someone asked him if he was English, he allegedly answered: 'Au contraire!'. In an interview given to the *Sunday Times* in 1964, he said: 'I hated London . . . everyone knew I was Irish – the taxi drivers called me Pat or Mick.'[24] In other words, he did not choose to submit to the English ascendancy and aesthetic either. His passion for the theatre did not lead him to identify with the great Irish figures in English drama, Wilde and Shaw, who (in Joyce's words) embodied the tradition of Irish 'jesters'.[25]

In London in these years, George Bernard Shaw (born in Dublin in 1856) was the great Irish figure, comparable to Yeats and likewise winner of the Nobel Prize for Literature two years after the Irish poet. Proving that he belonged to the same literary universe, Shaw signalled his opposition both to Yeats's folkloristic spiritualism in the name of reason and to Joyce's iconoclastic novelistic enterprise. Thus equidistant from Yeats and Joyce, he too sought to undermine British norms, while rejecting Irish national or nationalist values. *John Bull's Other Island* (1904) is the exemplar of a deliberately anti-Yeatsian play. A radical challenge to national clichés, through a simple inversion of the features of the stereotype it demonstrates that the Irishman of comedy is a creation of English folklore.

Shaw equally opposed Joyce's literary project and offered what was (to say the least) ambiguous praise for *Ulysses*, in a letter addressed in 1921 to Sylvia Beach, who had asked him to participate in a subscription to enable publication of the book: 'Dear Madam, I have read several fragments of

Ulysses in its serial form. It is a revolting record of a disgusting phase of civilization . . . To you, possibly, it may appeal as art . . . but to me it is all hideously real'.[26] Thus, not only did Shaw refuse to elevate to the status of art a realist picture that seemed to him to contravene literary exigencies, but furthermore he challenged the specific artistic interest that he should attribute to it as an Irishman, refusing any sentimental national affiliation.

It was in the British capital that Beckett began to write his first novel, *Murphy*. Many studies have been devoted to this text and for the most part have stressed the philosophical content of the work, generally basing themselves on Beckett's reading and explicit quotations: Descartes, Berkeley, Leibniz, Spinoza. Yet what has been largely neglected is that *Murphy* also maps out the whole literary space as it appeared to Beckett in these years and the position within it that he assigned himself. The narrative is based on toings and froings between Dublin (plus Cork) and London; and on a traditional dramatic structure that relates the characters to one another on the basis of several triangular relationships. Murphy, a Dubliner settled in London, is in search of work and everyone is in search of Murphy. Cork (which represents the province of the province: 'I say you know what women are . . . or has your entire life been spent in Cork?')[27] and Dublin pursue him. Cork is Mr. Neary, who is in love with Miss Counihan, who is herself engaged to Murphy. Dublin is Wylie, who proposes to watch over the young lady while a certain Cooper will go to London. All these Irish people are gradually going to meet up and make the journey to London, only finally to discover Murphy's ashes there.

One of the issues in the novel is the breaking of national taboos, the desire to shock Dublin morality. Dublin is the place one departs from and leaves without regret; it is a metaphor for archaism. All Beckett's resentments against Dublin and the Irish – 'For an Irish girl Miss Counihan was quite exceptionally anthropoid'[28] – are summarized and assembled: denunciations of 'Gaels' and other Druidic poets – embodied by Ticklepenny, 'Pot Poet From the County of Dublin' and 'bulging with as many minor beauties from the gaelic prosodoturfy as could be sucked out a mug of Beamish's porter';[29] refusal of Catholic prudishness and moralistic censorship by allusions to a supposed version of the text in Anglo-Irish, object of all the author's solicitude, in order to avoid the anathemas of Irish Catholic censorship. Celtic national mythology itself is directly challenged by what for the 1930s was an extremely violent blasphemy:

In Dublin a week later . . . Neary . . . was recognized . . . in the General Post Office, contemplating from behind the statue of Cuchulain. Neary had bared his head, as though the holy ground meant something to him. Suddenly he flung aside his hat, sprang forward, seized the dying hero by the thighs and began to dash his head against his buttocks, such as they are.[30]

As has been said, Cuchulain was one of Ireland's mythical heroes. Restored to honour by Yeats in particular, he was the embodiment of national ire and independence. A statue of him was erected to commemorate the famous 1916 rising and capture of Dublin's General Post Office. Beckett's friend A. J. Leventhal recounts:

[Beckett] sent me a post-card [from London]. Would I go to the post office in Dublin and measure the distance between the ground and Cuchulain's backside? . . . A crowd surrounded me while I knelt with a tape measure in hand to carry out my assignment and I had the good fortune to retire without being arrested [which is what almost happens to Beckett's protagonist]. It was essential for our author, who neglected nothing, to know whether this provocative gesture could actually be made.[31]

It was a highly subversive scene, therefore, directly in the tradition inaugurated by O'Casey, and whose violence must be appreciated if we are to interpret Beckett's novelistic project and his situation in the Irish literary space.

Murphy's will is a further mark of the very strong imprint of Dublin as seen from London:

With regard to the disposal of these my body, mind and soul, I desire that they be burnt and placed in a paper bag and brought to the Abbey Theatre, Lr Abbey Street, Dublin, and without pause into what the great and good Lord Chesterfield calls the necessary house, where their happiest hours have been spent, on the right as one goes down into the pit, and I desire that the chain be there pulled upon them, if possible during the performance of a piece, the whole to be executed without ceremony or show of grief.[32]

By taking the risk of ridiculing Ireland's most respected national institution, Beckett indicated the importance he attached to the Irish literary milieu, while alerting Londoners (publishers, potential critics, etc.) to his resolute attachment to a country that was now independent of England. His very insistence – the systematic, fanatical opposition – demonstrates that country's sway over him. Such was the utter ambiguity characteristic of Beckett in the 1930s: he did not succeed in jettisoning Ireland. Birthplace and home of his family, object of hatred and resentment, Dublin long remained the city from which he awaited recognition. Similarly, Beckett was unable to clarify his difficult, conflict-ridden, neurotic relations with his mother, despite psychoanalysis in London in these years, which calmed – or at least temporarily eased – his most painful psychosomatic symptoms (boils and convulsions). London appeared only to be a site of temporary asylum that enabled him, simply by virtue of distance, to accept his Dublin identity. (He would make several stays at his mother's during 1935, envisaging recommencing a career as a writer in Ireland.) A brief comparison between London and Paris illuminates the crucial distinction between asylum and exile, between departure for Paris and a still indecisive estrangement in London:

> By far the best part of the way was the toil from King's Cross up Caledonian Road, reminding him of the toil from St Lazare up Rue d'Amsterdam. And while Brewery Road was by no means a Boulevard de Clichy nor even des Batignoles, still it was better at the end of the hill than either of those, *as asylum (after a point) is better than exile.*[33]

The last chapter of *Murphy* is undoubtedly the most beautiful stylistically. It evokes a kind of ambiguous adieu to Ireland. Old Mr. Kelly, pushed by Celia, launches his kite, while she looks at the sky, 'simply to have that unction of soft sunless light on her eyes that was all she remembered of Ireland'.[34]

Two Irishmen in Paris

It was in Paris in 1928 that Beckett discovered Joyce, who for him was identified with the freedom afforded by this city. Beckett arrived in Paris as an English reader at the École Normale Supérieure on the rue d'Ulm and only frequented Irish and American exile circles. Thomas McGreevy, a Catholic characterized by 'rabid anti-British hostility',[35] and likewise an English reader at the École Normale, introduced him to Joyce, Sylvia Beach, Nancy Cunard, Richard Aldington and others. Beckett had read *Ulysses*, whose French translation, overseen by Larbaud, appeared the following year from Adrienne Monnier. Joyce was now famous in the intellectual coteries of English-speakers in Paris and elsewhere. Having rapidly become his 'secretary', Beckett took down Joyce's dictation of whole passages from *Work in Progress*. Witnesses relate Beckett's unbounded admiration for Joyce, his profound respect and total identification, which even extended to sartorial imitation.

He was very soon enlisted in his elder's war against his aesthetic opponents. In the first months of 1929 he wrote his first text for *Our Exagmination Round His Factification for Incamination of Work in Progress* – a collection dreamt up by Joyce in response to violent criticisms of *Work in Progress* (which was being published at the time in fragments in various journals under this generic title), and signed by twelve intimates or defenders of the Irish writer, including McGreevy and Eugene Jolas, each of whom was assigned his subject by Joyce. Knowing Beckett's competence in Italian and his good knowledge of *The Divine Comedy*, Joyce charged him with explaining his relationship to the oeuvre of Dante and that of Vico and Bruno. They agreed on the title of this short text – 'Dante . . . Bruno. Vico . . . Joyce' – with which the volume opened, in order to suggest the idea of an intellectual genealogy. In this first published text, Beckett immediately situated himself in the Joycean tradition with this strange introductory sentence: 'And now here I am, with my handful of abstractions, among which notably: a mountain, the coincidence of contraries, the inevitability of cyclic evolution, a system of Poetics, and the prospect of self-extension in the world of Mr Joyce's *Work in Progress*.'[36]

At the same time, in collaboration with Alfred Péron, whom he had met at Trinity College Dublin (TCD) some years earlier, Beckett worked on a French translation, commissioned by Joyce, of *Anna Livia Plurabelle* – one of the most famous sections of *Work in Progress*. The text satisfied Joyce, who was on the point of sending it to the printer for the next issue of the *Nouvelle Revue Française*, when he happened to show it to three of his friends, Philippe Soupault, Paul Léon and Ivan Goll. Beckett and Péron's text was gradually thrown into question, reworked, and completely revised with the author's collaboration. It would appear in May 1931 in volume nineteen of the *Nouvelle Revue Française* under the signatures of Samuel Beckett, Alfred Péron, Ivan Goll, Eugène Jolas, Paul-L. Léon, Adrienne Monnier and Philippe Soupault, 'in collaboration with the author'.[37] Whatever, it was at this time that Beckett became very familiar and even intimately acquainted with Joyce's literary project and creative processes. All the poems he published at the time in various American reviews in Paris openly identified with Joyce. Beckett even sent Samuel Putnam, an American who directed the review *This Quarter* with Edward Titus, a biographical note that he had written himself:

> Samuel Beckett is the most interesting of the younger Irish writers. He is a graduate of Trinity College, Dublin, and has lectured at the École Normale Supérieure in Paris. He has a great knowledge of Romance literature, is a friend of Rudmose-Brown and of Joyce, and has adopted the Joyce method to his poetry with original results. His impulse is lyric, but has been deepened through this influence and the influence of Proust and the historic method.[38]

Peggy Guggenheim recounts that during his second stay in Paris (from 1937) Beckett expressed his admiration for Céline's *Voyage au bout de la nuit*, but immediately made it clear that 'Joyce was the master, there was no one equal to him. He existed on one plane in literature, alone and incomparable. It was on the next lower plane, where everyone else existed, that Céline was the greatest.'[39]

The literary break made by James Joyce was the final stage in the constitution of the Irish literary space. Basing himself on the literary projects, debates and methods in play, Joyce invented and asserted a well-nigh absolute literary autonomy. In this highly politicized space, and counter to the dynamic of the Irish Revival which threatened to become (according to his expression in *Ulysses*) 'much too Irish', he imposed an aesthetic autonomy. This new position derived from a double refusal: a violent refusal of English literary norms, but also a refusal of the aesthetic dictates of the nationalist literature that was being constituted. Joyce moved beyond this simplistic alternative. In one and the same move, he denounced the 'nationalist mentality', literature invaded by 'the enthusiast and the doctrinaire'[40] – those who 'surrender to the trolls' by allowing Irish theatre to become 'the property of the rabblement of the most belated race in Europe'[41] – and, on the other side, 'court jesters' to the English.

It was through a subversive use of the language, and the national and social codes bound up with it, that Joyce invented literary modernity. In his fashion he took up the debate, which had exercised Irish literary circles throughout the nineteenth century, over whether Irish national culture worthy of the name could survive in English – that is, for the Irish and in their terms, in the language of the colonizer – or whether the imperative was to devote one's energies to reviving Gaelic. The literary enterprise of Yeats and his companions was in fact contested by those who wished to put an end to the cultural ascendancy of the language of the English colonizer. The declared aim of the Gaelic League (*Conradh na Gaeilge*), set up in 1893, was to suppress English in Ireland when British troops were expelled from it and to reintroduce the Gaelic language, whose use had virtually disappeared since the late eighteenth century – other than in a few remote regions – in favour of English. The discussions and debates on the relative merits of the two cultural options (English or Gaelic) continued for a long time. They profoundly marked the whole founding phase of Irish literature, perpetuating the division and rivalries between the 'celticizing Irish' and the 'anglicizing Irish'.[42] The former, who were more political, first of all carried out the technical task of establishing grammatical and orthographic norms for Gaelic; the latter produced strictly literary oeuvres that rapidly achieved widespread recognition in London literary circles.

Joyce's literary project went beyond this alternative and rested on a highly subtle Irish re-appropriation of the English language. He disarticulated the language of colonization by integrating elements from all the European languages into it, but also by undermining the norms of British propriety and employing, in conformity with his national tradition, the registers of the obscene or the scatological. Ridiculing the English tradition enabled him to make this language of domination, once subverted, a quasi-foreign language in *Finnegans Wake*. In this way he sought to overturn the hierarchy between London and Dublin, to turn its own norms against English, and to restore to Ireland a language that was specific to it.

By refusing the aesthetic writ of both London and Dublin, Joyce was to produce an Irish literature in an assumed extra-territoriality. It was in Paris, a politically neutral site and international literary capital, that he sought to establish this seemingly contradictory position, which is ex-centric in the full sense of the word. In his essay on English literature, Cyril Connolly, a

writer and critic of Irish extraction, explains the respective places of Paris
and Dublin in the literary war launched against London:

> The second quarter was Paris which held in the attack on the new
> Mandarins the line taken by Dublin against their predecessors thirty
> years before. It was here that conspirators met in Sylvia Beach's little
> bookshop where *Ulysses* lay stacked like dynamite in a revolutionary
> cellar and then scattered down the Rue de l'Odéon on the missions
> assigned to them.[43]

Such was the literary configuration from which Irish literature was
henceforth to be written. The literary triangle formed by the three capitals
– Dublin, London, Paris – which encapsulates the whole Irish literary
universe at the point when Beckett embarked on a literary career, is
profoundly inscribed in the thinking and vision of Irish writers. Thus,
Seamus Heaney, Noble Prize winner for Literature in 1995, who was born
in 1939 in the North of Ireland and was a lecturer for some years in Belfast
where he studied, and who provoked a scandal in his own country by
settling near Dublin, precisely refers to the same oppositions in order to
describe the options available to him:

> If, like Joyce and Beckett, I had gone to live in Paris, I would simply
> have been conforming to a cliché. If I had left for London, that
> would have been regarded as an ambitious move but a normal one.
> But to go to Wicklow was a highly significant act . . . As soon as I
> crossed the border, my private life fell into the public domain and
> newspapers wrote editorials on my gesture. A weird paradox![44]

Today, we should add to this configuration New York, which through the
US Irish community contributes significantly to the international recognition of Irish writers.

To understand Beckett's identification with Joyce, and discern the form
of his itinerary, it is necessary to stress their real proximity and the
parallelism – in some respects one might almost even speak of a superimposition at a distance of twenty years – of their itineraries, choices and
battles.

Political and Literary Uses of Dante

While Joyce made a massive contribution to fashioning Irish literature such as Beckett discovered it at the end of the 1920s, their enthusiasms and rejections were exactly the same. Their extolling of Dante and distrust of, or sarcastic remarks about, the Celtic prophets took virtually the same form. We cannot say that one of them – the younger – relied on the other to guide and justify his tastes and distastes. Rather, because at the age of twenty Beckett found himself in the same frame of mind, he was going to explore the same type of response. And we should hear Beckett's diatribes from the 1930s as an echo of Joyce's violent attacks on Yeats's theatrical choices at the Abbey in 1901: 'an aesthete has a floating will, and Mr. Yeats [has a] treacherous instinct of adaptability . . . the Irish literary theatre by its surrender to the trolls has cut itself adrift from the line of advancement.'[45]

Aside from political passions, which were bound up with their respective social affiliations and radically differentiated them – Beckett, who claimed to be apolitical, came from a Protestant family enriched over two generations by business and trade, while Joyce belonged to the highly politicized Catholic petty bourgeoisie – the two men made the same kind of intellectual choices. Just as Joyce at University College Dublin[46] had chosen to study the languages and literatures that would enable him to master French, Italian, German and Norwegian, Beckett very early on specialized in the study of foreign languages – especially French, Italian, German and Spanish.[47]

Trinity College Dublin was 'the educational and spiritual home of the Protestant Ascendancy',[48] the institution where for more than three centuries the Protestant elite sent sons destined for brilliant careers. Sean O'Casey, a Protestant autodidact and nationalist activist, captured Dublin's respect for this summit of Protestant culture in a phrase, calling it in his memoirs 'the temple of learning'.[49] Beckett entered TCD in October 1923, two years after the proclamation of Irish independence and a few months after the end of the terrible civil war. There, naturally, little nationalist enthusiasm and proselytism was to be encountered, since people were still loyal to the British Crown. Instead, as might be imagined, Beckett discovered an atmosphere marked by a completely new political situation.

Beckett's decision to study foreign languages and literature was uncommon. In this nationalist context, at a time when debates in Dublin revolved around the issue of whether to advocate isolationism or cosmo-

politanism in cultural matters and, further, whether to revert to Gaelic as
the national language or accept English, the choice of a cosmopolitan
culture open to the world was already deliberately political, if only in its
indifference. But Beckett's a-politicism as a sports-playing young bourgeois, a total stranger to the nationalist problem – something that distinguished him from Joyce, who was impassioned by the national question
– does not mean that he was not already in the position of a double refusal.
He refused the social position intended for him by his father, who was
convinced that after brilliant university studies Beckett would succeed him
at the head of his business; he also rejected the set of questions posed to him
by the national intellectual universe in which he developed.

That is why the two writers' shared interest in Dante is the most
convincing proof of their common assertion of literature's autonomy.
Joyce's passion for Dante, whom he read in the original and never stopped
quoting, was as precocious and enduring as Beckett's. At the age of
eighteen, Joyce was nicknamed 'the Dante of Dublin' by Olivier Go-
garty;[50] and every significant occasion in his life would serve as a pretext for
flattering comparisons with the author of *The Divine Comedy*. He very early
on made reference to Dante's exile to explain his own situation and, when
he began composing *Ulysses*, prided himself on the fact that he was the
same age as the Florentine writer when he started *The Divine Comedy*.
Beckett likewise initiated himself at a very young age into the subtleties of
Dante's oeuvre. In his third year at Trinity College he attended Rudmose-
Brown's lectures on *The Divine Comedy* and worked in particular on the
fifth canto of *Purgatorio*. For him too, Dante's exile was a reason, often
acknowledged, for identification.[51]

Dante was therefore their first intellectual bond, the first indication of a
common endeavour to escape from what they felt was the fate of Irish
confinement, a sign of cosmopolitan inclinations, the mark of an identical
refusal of a purely nationalist aesthetic, which they alone could detect in
one another when they met in Paris. To identify with Dante as a literary
master was, without even explaining it, to convey the non-national
character of literature; without stating it, it was a refusal to submit
exclusively to Yeatsian poetic dogma.

That is why the first text published by Beckett was also a defence and
illustration of Joyce with the weapons of Dante ('Dante . . . Bruno.
Vico . . . Joyce'). In it Beckett summarized and theorized their common
literary position (or literary politics). Elevated, highly argued references

helped him to justify Joyce's literary project in both its strictly formal
dimension and its specifically political implications. He began with a
summary of the theses of the Neapolitan philosopher regarding the
evolution of civilizations, language and poetry. Joyce, he argued, had
returned via Vico to a poetic primitivism, a kind of raw material of poetry
forgotten by civilization:

> Mr Joyce has desophisticated language. And it is worth while
> remarking that no language is so sophisticated as English. It is
> abstracted to death . . . This writing that you find so obscure is a
> quintessential extraction of language and painting and gesture, with
> all the inevitable clarity of the old inarticulation. Here is the savage
> economy of hieroglyphics. Here words are not the contortions of
> 20th century printer's ink. They are alive.
>
> And if you don't understand it, Ladies and Gentlemen, it is because
> you are too decadent to receive it. Here form *is* content, content *is*
> form. You complain that this stuff is not written in English. It is not
> written at all. It is not to be read – or rather it is not only to be read. It
> is to be looked at and listened to. His writing is not *about* something;
> *it is that something itself.* [52]

This identification with a literary object that is completely novel because it
is in itself, as a form, a visible, palpable *thing*; and this assertion of a literary
'savagery', or 'barbarism', are a different way – more subtle and more noble
– of re-appropriating the mythological discourse of the Celtic foundations
of Irish poetry and belief in a 'pure', specific origin. But above all they are
an affirmation and precise explanation of Joyce's programme for disarti-
culating the English language. The mythical primitiveness of poetry that
Joyce is said to have rediscovered against the empty decadence of civilization is, obviously, a challenge to the codes of English literary propriety.

The text proceeds in the form of a highly sophisticated, euphemized
anti–English manifesto and an attack on the 'gaelicizing' Irish that sum-
marize the complexity of Joyce's position. Beckett constructs a kind of
instrument of war against the sway of English over literature, in order to
justify and dignify Joyce's simultaneously literary, linguistic and political
project. It involves a veritable syllogism that can be broken down as
follows:

They [Dante and Joyce] both saw how worn out and threadbare was the conventional language of cunning literary artificers, both rejected an approximation to a universal language. If English is not yet so definitely a polite necessity as Latin was in the Middle Ages, at least one is justified in declaring that its position in relation to other European languages is to a great extent that of mediaeval Latin to the Italian dialect.[53]

In other words, English now occupied in Europe the place of Latin during the Middle Ages — that is, the dominant, unchallenged position of a vehicle of trans-national communication. And English, like Latin in the fourteenth century, was an old, not to say dead, language.[54]

Dante, Beckett observed,

did not adopt the vulgar out of any kind of local jingoism nor out of any determination to assert the superiority of Tuscan to all its rivals as a form of spoken Italian. On reading his *De Vulgari Eloquentia* we are struck by his complete freedom from civic intolerance. He attacks the world's Portadownians: '*Nam quicumque tam obscenae rationis est, ut locum suae nationis delitioissimum credat esse sub sole, hic etiam prae cunctis proprium vulgarae licitur, idest maternam locutionem. Nos autem, cui mundus est patria . . .*'[55]

In other words, explaining Dante's theses allowed Beckett to contest the sway of the Irish cultural nationalism that was seeking to impose the use of Gaelic on all intellectuals. Dante's option for the vernacular, he explained, was not dictated by chauvinistic considerations; Dante was not seeking to advance the Tuscan language. And in order to clarify his target, Beckett introduced Portadown, a small town in Northern Ireland, thus overturning the habitual presuppositions of commentary on literary classics. Beckett updates, 'Irishes', and hence politicizes Dante's text: 'Portadownians' are (Irish) symbols of the parochial mindset. As can be seen, the sophistication and complexity of the argument make it possible to hold together the two refusals that were constitutive of Joyce's position: refusal of a straightforward use of English, which would be submission to the English colonial order; but at the same time refusal of the nationalist archaism that a literary use of Gaelic would represent.

'His conclusion,' Beckett continued,

is that the corruption common to all the dialects makes it impossible to select one rather than another as an adequate literary form, and that he who would write in the vulgar must assemble the purest elements from each dialect and construct a synthetic language that would at least possess more than a circumscribed local interest . . . He wrote a vulgar that *could* have been spoken by an ideal Italian who had assimilated what was best in all the dialects of his country, but which in fact was certainly not spoken nor ever had been.[56]

Consequently, like Dante, who against Latin had chosen Italian dialects without privileging any one of them – his own – by regarding it as superior to the others, and who had assembled elements from a variety of languages, Joyce against English undertook to write a new language, a synthesis of several other languages, without privileging his own dialect: Gaelic.

The Joycean 'explosive' of which Connolly speaks is here justified in all its dimensions and dignified by the comparison with Dante. Beckett, who himself concocted this impeccable syllogism, transfigured the Irish linguistic and political debate by resorting to the noblest of texts. The historical and intellectual parallelism finds all its force in a kind of updating of the inextricably literary and political problematic established by Dante. By restoring a political, subversive power to a text that is ordinarily precluded from historicization by its very status as a literary classic, Beckett succeeded in defending Joyce's autonomous options, while demonstrating their political resonance. But if Beckett defended the position and choices of James Joyce with as much intelligence and sophistication, it was doubtless because he was one of the very few capable of understanding the enormous literary revolution set in train by his compatriot.

The Irish Purgatory

Strangely enough, for both Joyce and Beckett reference to *The Divine Comedy* was also a different way, ennobling and unexpected, of evoking Ireland. Historically, *Purgatorio* is an unanticipated literary metamorphosis of Ireland. When Purgatory was 'invented' in the twelfth century, several founding texts, including *The Purgatory of Saint Patrick* by the Cistercian monk H. de Saltrey, located it in Ireland, in a deserted spot, in the form of a round, dark hole which St. Patrick made penitents descend into to be 'purged of all [their] sins'.[57] We know that the success of this text was immediate and considerable; that it was 'one of the bestsellers of the Middle Ages', as Jacques Le Goff notes;[58] and that it remained famous up until the eighteenth century. So well-known was it that Rabelais and Ariosto referred to it, Shakespeare evoked it in *Hamlet*, Calderon explicitly made it the theme of one of his plays – *The Purgatory of Saint Patrick* – and Dante himself obviously studied it very closely.[59] A little later, a precise geographical location was indicated for the Irish Purgatory: Station Island on the Lough Derg in County Donegal. At the end of the twelfth century, a chapel was built on this site and a pilgrimage instituted that survived destruction and proscription. The island would become a summit of Irish Catholicism and, with the aid of St. Patrick's 'nationalization', was rapidly linked with nationalist demonstrations and fervour. A new church dedicated to St. Patrick was finished in 1931 and 'every year some 15,000 pilgrims visit the site between June 1 and August 15'.[60]

Thus, Ireland embodies one of the greatest Western religious and literary mythologies. Beckett (like Joyce) worked from this strange coincidence, which transformed his native island into a Dantesque territory, his country into a formidable fiction, his 'disinherited' land into a quintessentially literary reason for hope. In Dante, Purgatory is an island that takes the form of a mountain. In Beckett's first texts, as a matter of good logic, it is therefore Ireland as a whole that is assimilated to Purgatory – an unavowed way of putting Ireland at the centre of his writings while circumventing national poetic imperatives, whether Celtic or realist, and obeying the injunctions of Joyce himself, who advised young writers not to abandon their national tradition.[61]

Thus ennobled, Ireland becomes an ex-territorialized territory, a utopian place, without reference-points or history. Recourse to Dante is a magnificent way of cocking a snook at politicians and writers, a literary weapon against national realism, and a way of appropriating Catholic and nationalist dogma. It was precisely with a comparison between Dante's *Purgatorio* and Joyce's that Beckett concluded 'Dante . . . Bruno. Vico . . . Joyce', allowing him to clarify his iconoclastic (because literary) conception of Purgatory. 'Conical' in Dante, 'spherical' in Joyce, Purgatory is, in a third term making it possible to reconcile opposites, 'a flood of movement and vitality' according to Beckett.[62] This dynamic conception cleverly overturns the most traditional literary and metaphysical presuppositions. Just as he had gone beyond the nationalist alternative by inventing a new aesthetic position, Joyce, as theorized by Beckett, transcended the simple alternative, laid down by Catholic morality, between good and evil. In so doing, he broke new ground, proposing a literature of movement, a novel aesthetic dynamic.

Dante's *Purgatorio* has become a kind of reference-point and literary model for Irish writers who refuse the national, popular, Celtic conception of poetry. It embodies a different poetic genealogy, one that is older, more noble and equally 'legitimate'. Seamus Heaney has adopted it in turn, thus in a sense becoming the poet of the third Dantesque generation in Ireland.[63] Taking the same road as Joyce and Beckett, he has translated extracts from *The Divine Comedy*, including the Ugolino episode. His poem 'Station Island', which supplies the title of one of his collections,[64] is a (quasi-) quotation from Dante, underscored by the very form of the poem, the dialogue structure of the verses and the apostrophe to characters. As in *The Divine Comedy*, the ghosts of dead friends appear to the poet, among them the tutelary figure of Joyce. With Heaney, Ireland continues the literary transfiguration started by Yeats and continued by Joyce and Beckett. By way of those who looked for specific tools to contest the sway of the national vision of literature, Dante has become one of the founding fathers of Irish literature.

Only this literary constellation can explain Beckett's constant recourse to Dante's text in his first works of fiction. This literary rendition of Ireland supplied him with a substratum, a grid for interpreting the world, an inexhaustible reservoir of metaphors and learned allusions, and became a motor of literary creation. *The Divine Comedy* is a prodigious palimpsest, a founding text, that is quoted, parodied, corrupted, appropriated.

Perhaps his own theorization of Joyce's project gave Beckett the impetus to the poetry in motion that marks all his early texts. Just as throughout *The Divine Comedy* Dante himself proceeds at the pace of the specific dynamic of his journey in the beyond – 'We climbed within the cloven rock, and the surface on each side pressed close on us and the ground beneath required both hands and feet . . . "Do not fall back a step; still make thy way up the mountain behind me till some wise guide appear for us." ';[65] and just as Joyce's *Ulysses* proceeds at the pace of Leopold Bloom's steps tramping the streets of Dublin, Beckett's writing (until *Murphy* at least) is also constructed 'on the move'. In both his poems and his early fiction (*More Pricks than Kicks*), Beckett mimes Dante's journey to Hell and Bloom's in Dublin, starting out from the same setting and according to the same dynamic. Or rather, he uses this model to impart literary form to the instability that characterizes his narrator[66] – his irrepressible capacity to move, walk, go round in circles, never to come to a halt, as if nowhere offered him asylum.

And that is why multiplying direct homages to Dante in his texts is another way for Beckett to pledge aesthetic and stylistic allegiance to Joyce; to remain (as he had put it in *Our Exagmination*) in the 'prospect of self-extension in the world of Mr Joyce's *Work in Progress*'.[67] It is also a tacit means of stating his ethical debt and dependence – in other words, of ranging himself on the side of literary autonomy and protesting against the political (national) dependence of literature. This is one way of understanding the acknowledgement of a debt confided to Lawrence Harvey in the 1960s: Joyce had taught him the 'integrity of literature'.

The central character in his first fictional narrative, *Dream of Fair to Middling Women* (1932), taken up again in the collection of short stories that was to follow – *More Pricks than Kicks* (published in London in 1934) – where Beckett reused virtually the same narrative material, is called Belacqua. He is taken directly from Dante, who classes him among the 'nonchalant', the indolent, the 'eternal waiters' of Ante-Purgatory:

> We went over [to a great boulder], and there were people there resting in the shade behind the rock as men settle to rest through indolence, and one of them, who seemed to me weary, sat clasping his knees and holding his face low between them.
>
> 'O my dear Lord,' I said 'cast thine eye on him there who shows himself more indolent than if sloth were his sister.'
>
> . . .
>
> His lazy movements and curt speech moved my lips a little to a smile, then I began: 'Belacqua, I am not grieved for thee henceforth. But tell me, why art thou seated here? Does thou wait for escort, or has thou only resumed the old ways?'[68]

The surname of a Florentine craftsman, who sculpted lute and guitar necks and was known for his indolence and taste for drink, Belacqua is therefore the explicit identifying figure whom Beckett has chosen – an image of the nonchalance, indolence and passivity of one condemned to wait for the equivalent of his lifetime. But he is also the character of the most paradoxical irony in Dante's whole trilogy. The poet-narrator begins to 'smile' when he comes across a Belacqua sparing in his gestures and words, who hails him by sarcastically querying the words of Virgil himself, assuring the poet that they will only have to rest when they have reached the peak of the mountain of Purgatory: ' "there look to rest thy weariness." . . . And as soon as he had spoken these words, a voice sounded close by: "Perhaps before then thou wilt have need of a seat." '[69]

Belacqua's omnipresence in the first stories has of course been highlighted by Beckett criticism. In 1959 Walter A. Strauss stressed that this character from Dante is the first of the whole long series of Beckett bums, as did Alfred Simon subsequently.[70] But this evident choice has never been related to an aesthetic position – Beckett's position in the Irish literary space. In the first short story in *More Pricks than Kicks*, 'Dante and the Lobster', Beckett represents Belacqua as a translator who, in the course of an Italian lecture, ponders the transcription of *qui vive la pieta quando è ben morta* . . .;[71] in 'Ding-Dong' Belacqua meets a woman who quite explicitly evokes Dante's Beatrice and sells 'seats in heaven . . . tuppence apiece, four fer a tanner': 'The features were null, only luminous, impassive and secure, petrified in radiance, or words to that effect, for the reader is requested to note that this sweet style is Belacqua's . . . The implications of this triumphant figure, the just and the unjust, etc., are better forgone.'[72] This ironic reprise of Dante's *dolce stil nuovo*, signalled as a literary, parodic effect, gives a good idea of the tone of these short stories. Belacqua explicitly reappears in *Murphy* ('[a]t this moment Murphy would willingly have waived his expectation of Ante-Purgatory for five minutes in his chair, renounced the lee of Belacqua's rock and his embryonal repose, looking down at dawn across the reeds to the trembling of the austral sea and the sun obliquing to the north as it rose').[73] And he also features in many of the ensuing texts: *Watt, Molloy, Malone Dies, Waiting for Godot, Endgame, How It Is*. Beckett would long remember Dante's smile, which we encounter once again in *The Lost Ones* and then *Company*: 'So sat waiting to be purged the old lutist cause of Dante's first quarter-smile'.[74]

'Home Olga' (Continuation and Conclusion)

The whole Irish literary space, such as it has just been evoked, was present, albeit in euphemized, hermetic form, in the poem 'Home Olga'. All the allusions, quotations, references and parodies in this text are determined by Irish literary history, including the learned references to Dante, which are neither pure nor literary, but pertain to a 'literary politics'. Under Beckett's pen, Dante became a weapon in the struggle against literary nationalism. And we cannot claim to be able to decipher via a purely internal reading a poem that, in appearance at least, actually makes so little reference to the world. In an odd way, history (simultaneously and inseparably literary and political) has proved capable of providing new instruments for deciphering this hermetic text, to which accordingly we can now return.

In particular, the importance of Dante in Beckett's aesthetic universe makes it possible to offer a different interpretation of the literary appropriation of the three theological virtues in the poem.[75] The strange presence, insistent and precious, of this chromatic symbolism can be understood by referring to Dante's *Purgatorio*, where the three theological virtues, signalled by their simple colour or represented metaphorically by 'ladies' in different colours, appear on numerous occasions.[76] Once again Dante mediates the relationship with Joyce. In this way, in 'Home Olga' Beckett asserts Joyce's identification with Dante: the literally translated *dolce stil nuovo* is applied to the project of his elder, 'the sweet noo style'.

By using Joyce's initials not only at the beginning of the line, but also twice in internal rhymes, Beckett offers ironic proof of his technical mastery, of his distant intimacy with the oeuvre. But he also evokes in the most elliptical fashion Joyce's whole mental and literary universe: 'Home Olga' is a *catalogue raisonné* of Joyce's oeuvre. The fifth line – 'Swoops and loops . . . and view of the mew' is an allusion to Dedalus, 'the high-flying experimenter' in *Portrait of the Artist*; 'the tip of a friendly yiddophile' is a precise reference to Joyce's definition of God as a collector of foreskins in *Ulysses*; the veiled reference 'adieu, adieu, adieu' is not only to Stephen, associated with his 'cunning', but also (according to Harvey) a homage to Joyce's earliest texts, *Chamber Music*, published in 1907, and to one of his favourite songs.[77] The eighth line is an extraordinary contraction of *Finnegans Wake*, an explanation of the book's temporal disruption, repeated in the Italian expression 'Che sarà sarà fu' in the subsequent line, which underscores Joyce's polyglottism.

Parodying it, Beckett also takes up an expression of Joyce's in *Anna Livia Plurabelle* that could have been directly addressed to him, and which accounts for their relationship, built in part for Joyce on Beckett's belonging to the Irish academic nobility: 'Latin me that me Trinity Scholard'. Beckett re-appropriates it as a sign of complicity and friendship, transforming it into 'riddle me that my rapparee' – an impertinent way of ironizing about Joyce's methods.

Thus for Beckett, Joyce became an inimitable, unsurpassable model aesthetically and formally – a kind of intimate, intimately known opponent who sought to enlist him as official propagandist. 'Home Olga' marks the moment of his break: in order to find his own literary way, Beckett also had to struggle against Joyce's sway. Joyce had opened up an aesthetic royal road, but immediately closed it, by condemning those who wished to follow him to mere imitation.

A poem of homage and leave-taking ('Ecce himself and the pickthank agnus'), 'Home Olga' is a summary of all the contradictions Beckett found himself trapped in at the beginning of the 1930s. There is no doubt that Beckett was the person who best understood both Joyce's work and the reasons for his stylistic and political choices: telling of Ireland outside the canons established by Ireland; and choosing exile in order to tell of it. Having experienced them himself, he was intimately acquainted with the impasses in which Joyce found himself in Dublin. Above all, better than anyone else he knew the weight of literary censorship, the stylistic alternative imposed on Irish writers: symbolism or realism. He knew that the only literary road he could take was the one Joyce had opened – and closed – for him. For a long time Beckett would find it impossible to hit on a literary solution of his own.

For close on fifteen years, oscillating between deliberate imitation and affected liberation, Beckett was going to seek his way, at once with and against this genius at improvization, who integrated all extraneous elements into his prose and made use of the aleatory. His own literary labour was a long search for an exit: at the point when he understood that Joyce had found the only aesthetic solution that suited him, and occupied the only possible position for someone wishing to demonstrate the full, total autonomy of literature to maximum effect, Beckett discovered that any naïve access to literature was, by the same token, closed to him. Joyce simultaneously provided and prevented access to the road of formalism, to the subversion of the codes of literary propriety, to the struggle against realist conformism, to the refusal of Catholic and nationalist conformism. From his first stay in Paris, Beckett understood the terrifying contradiction he found himself trapped in. He was immediately placed in an untenable position, between the imitation that destroyed him as an artist and an impossible break.

3

Philosophical Motifs

Back in Dublin, the problems started. Caught up in painful contradictions, at once neurotic, political and literary, which he would spend nearly fifteen years resolving, and tied hand and foot by a kind of double bind that rendered 'domestication' and exile equally painful and desirable, Beckett could not decide either to return or to depart.

Aside from a brief stay in London (in 1935), he sank slowly and consciously into decline and self-destruction. His letters to, among others, Thomas McGreevy, with whom he remained in contact by letter until his death in 1967, attest to it. He was 'doped and buttoned up in sadness', '[a]n insensible mass of alcohol, nicotine, and feminine intoxication. A heap of guts. With no end for.'[1] Beckett became the 'family idiot', the black sheep of a bourgeois family that sought to conceal the vices of a hopeless case from the gaze of the world. Branded, pointed at, marginal in a prudish society, and unable to bear the burden of the fault for which he was blamed, he slowly destroyed himself. On 8 October 1932 he wrote to his friend Georges Reavey in Paris: 'I'll be here till I die, creeping along genteel roads on a stranger's bike.'[2] He referred to his relationship with an abusive mother who made him feel guilty, and who made every effort to integrate him socially and professionally into Ireland, so that he would stay with her: 'which I suppose [if it] all boils down to saying what a bad son I am, then amen. It is a title for me of as little honour as infamy.'[3] In June 1937 he once again wrote: 'This morning Mother urged me to apply for the post of assistant librarian in the National Library, at £150 a year, assuring me that my ignorance of Gaelic was of no significance.'[4] The power of the Catholic, national and linguistic order established since the advent of independence exacerbated his maladjustment and anger.

Nevertheless, he sought by all possible means to find an Irish literary road, a variety of formal compromise that did not force him into Gaelic aesthetics and yet did not condemn him to post-Joycean sterility. While invoking his 'verbal constipation' in correspondence with McGreevy, as if Joyce's censorship was so strong that it literally prevented him from writing, he composed extremely hermetic occasional poems.[5] The themes of treason and impasse are dominant in them and they seem to amount to the systematic exploration – in a disavowed, sublimated and intellectualized form – of a simultaneously formal, thematic and geographical solution to his painful situation of internal exile. A number of these texts were also written in memory of his father, who died abruptly in 1933, and to whom he was very close. Their manifest setting is Dublin and its immediate environs and they are inscribed in a kind of circular itinerary, labyrinth or prison of the city and the surrounding hills. Some, like the poem entitled 'Sanies I', which evokes a bicycle ride in the Dublin countryside, are constructed in motion, like an attempt at evasion or exile, a metaphorical, futile return journey.[6] 'Enueg II', written in 1932 as he resigned his teaching post at Trinity College, is a perfect illustration of his painful, undecidable situation:

> sweating like Judas
> tired of dying
> tired of policemen
> feet in marmalade
> perspiring profusely
> heart in marmalade [7]

All his choices made him seem a traitor in his own eyes. Protestant in a Catholic Ireland; intellectual in a bourgeois business family that pressurized him to conform to type; resigner from the most prestigious academic institution of his country; ill at ease and unconventional in Dublin's artistic and intellectual circles; nostalgic for Parisian life; a poet refusing the Yeatsian road that was quasi-mandatory in Dublin in the 1930s – always 'displaced', Beckett began to drink, fell ill, became a down-and-out, shut himself up at home, and gradually acquired all the symptoms of impotence and depression. He was a traitor to the family order, the educational order, the social order and the artistic order.

Apart from a rage that was more mocking than militant, there was nothing to supply him with material for possible composition. He was in the strange position of someone who wanted to write but without knowing what: any idea of a 'message' had been devalued by the 'bardolatry' that for him, as for Joyce, had ruined any attempt at naïve narration, lyrical or realist, for a long time to come. But no alternative seemed conceivable, since the initiative in formal construction had been seized by Joyce. Beckett's despair, in these years at least, stemmed from a sense of having arrived too late.

Contrary to Joyce, who invented and established his position as an exile and a revolutionary, original form on his own, Beckett had to break new ground beyond a point of no return. Political messages were used and worn out, Celtic watchwords hackneyed, the literary revolution already accomplished. From the retrospect of the 1960s, when he replied to Lawrence Harvey's questions, Beckett never stopped repeating the emptiness of these years. He described his poems of the 1930s as 'the work of a very young man with nothing to say and the itch to make'.[8] Harvey adds that Beckett deplored their stiltedness and exhibition of literary and artistic erudition, which he characterized as a pose; and explained that he spent the years following his resignation from Trinity College Dublin (in December 1931) 'not knowing what to do'.[9] We find a direct, decisive echo of these years in *Krapp's Last Tape*: 'Nothing to say, not a squeak';[10] and in the first lines of *Waiting for Godot*, which is to be read as a very painful, specific interrogation of the writing to come, directions for the use of Beckett's whole oeuvre from 1945 onwards:

ESTRAGON: (*giving up again*). Nothing to be done.
VLADIMIR: . . . I'm beginning to come round to that opinion. All my life I've tried to put it from me, saying, Vladimir, be reasonable, you haven't yet tried everything. And I resumed the struggle.[11]

'Old Geulincx, Dead Young'

In these years Geulincx became one of Beckett's major intellectual references.[12] His philosophy did not supply Beckett with a set of technical and conceptual tools, but – and this is very striking from the composition of *Murphy* onwards – a kind of intellectual justification or ennoblement of his strange, difficult relationship to the world. No doubt his speculative requirements could only be satisfied by this intellectualist scepticism. More than that, however, Geulincx's philosophy of constraint and impotence, of the utmost separation between world, body and mind, offered him an intellectual tool that would enable him to escape the contradiction he was caught in. He would not expatiate or comment on the disjunction between body and mind conceptualized by the 'minor Cartesian' Arnold Geulincx. He would use him in literary fashion to represent this extreme dualism and, on the basis of his own experience, would identify with Geulincx's occasionalism.

Experience, argued Geulincx, teaches me that 'my tongue moves around in my mouth when I want to speak; my arms stretch out and my feet advance when I want to walk, when I want to swim. But it is not me who creates this movement, for I do not know how it occurs.'[13] Given that body and mind are inseparable by nature, I do not know how I act on my body. I am ignorant of the mechanisms of a causality that can be attributed to neither body nor mind. God is what makes it possible to pass from a movement of the body to a modification of the soul and vice versa. The principle of externality or, rather, of the mutual foreignness of the world and myself ('on this stage I am merely a spectator, not an actor,' wrote Geulincx), involves a necessary passivity, a waiting-game, an action reduced to necessity. Hence the precept that recalls the limits of action and of the body: *Ubi nihil vales, ibi nihil velis* ('where you are worth nothing, you should want nothing'). And it was in an understanding of the set of constraints preventing any knowledge of things in themselves (*rem non esse ita in se, ut apprehenditur a nobis*), and limiting the principle of any action (*Quod nescis quomodo fiat, id non facis*: 'what you do not understand, you do not do'), that Beckett also discovered the only room for freedom permitted by Geulincx's pitiless system – the sole, paradoxical solution offered him in his corporeal, literary and national prison.

We frequently encounter this conception of a constrained freedom in Beckett. In particular, albeit in highly obscure fashion, he explained it in *Molloy*, on the basis of an image borrowed from Geulincx's *Ethics*: 'I who had loved the image of old Geulincx, dead young, who left me free, on the black boat of Ulysses, to crawl towards the East, along the deck. That is a great measure of freedom, for him who has not the pioneering spirit.'[14] This is in fact a specific allusion to a comparison made by Geulincx when explaining the paradoxical principle of freedom as he conceived it:

Is there something that prevents a passenger in a boat which is taking him westwards at great speed from heading eastwards in the boat? Thus it is that God's will directs all things, leads everything in a kind of impetuous fatality, but without anything standing in the way of what we attempted, in so far as it is in us to resist his will by full, perfectly free deliberation on our part.[15]

This strange, contradictory solution draws on Descartes and Leibniz as well as Spinoza. In cases of the most extreme compulsion, Geulincx granted a certain indetermination that is the sole tragic space of freedom – an intellectual, solitary and autarkic freedom giving access neither to the body nor to the world: 'The passenger can move about the boat. But the latter pursues its course regardless.'[16]

Beckett would seek to illustrate Geulincx's system of mutual externality very precisely, by conveying it in literary form with the introduction of the indolent, nonchalant character from Dante's *Purgatorio*, Belacqua. An exact embodiment of the principle of inaction stated by Geulincx, he also allowed Beckett to represent the main paradox of freedom under constraints: 'This was his Belacqua fantasy and perhaps the most highly systematized of the whole collection. It belonged to those that lay just beyond the frontiers of suffering, *it was the first landscape of freedom*.'[17] This novelistic use of Geulincx's idealist scepticism was neither formalist, nor directly literary: Beckett discovered in Geulincx's system a formulation of his own intellectual, national, literary, social and psychological confinement and a tool for understanding it. And that in turn enabled him to implement new narrative solutions.

The Coincidence of Contraries

In the course of his search for conceptual or aesthetic solutions, Beckett also managed to translate into literary, formal terms the insurmountable series of obstacles and constraints he came up against. From his first stories, he sought to exploit all dialectical figures, forms of compromise or 'coincidence of contraries'.

The first of these forms is rhetorical. In order to assimilate opposite, reputedly irreconcilable terms, Beckett privileges the figure of oxymoron, or the alliance of contrary terms ('[h]e had a strong weakness for oxymoron,' says the narrator of 'Ding-Dong', after relating one of his ' "moving pauses" '),[18] and that of antithesis. In *Dream of Fair to Middling Women*, he evokes the gap between words or between sentences, 'the antithetical seasons of words (nothing so simple as antithetical)'.[19]

The second form of coincidence of contraries employed by Beckett is literary: the figure of Purgatory, which is the synthesis and supersession of the opposition between good and evil. Intermediary between Paradise and Hell, waiting-site for Belacqua, Purgatory is also a border that makes it possible to rethink all overly simple alternatives, all the possibilities opened up by literature. In the undecidable, intolerable situation Beckett found himself in, the theoretical, geographical and literary middle term of Purgatory is what made it possible for him to prolong waiting, to defer choosing, to construct in his texts themselves the permanent aporia that always makes it possible to suspend decisions. Writing as Beckett then conceived it was precisely in the no-man's land of Purgatory, 'without the courage to end or the strength to go on'.[20]

Finally, the contradiction is resolved through a conceptual understanding of the contradiction itself in the privileged form of immobile motion. This immobile mobility, directly linked to the disjunction of soul and body, very precisely corresponds to the relative motion described by Geulincx; to the tiny room for manoeuvre granted, within constrained motion, to the one who has embarked on the boat of freedom à la Geulincx. It is sought after as a kind of miraculous equilibrium, of ataractic paradise incessantly disrupted by the sentence of perpetual motion. This bizarre, constant impulse is described in the form of a curse – that of a body condemned to circular, incessant motion if it wishes to escape the Furies:

> He was pleased to think that he could give what he called the Furies the slip by merely setting himself in motion . . . From the ingle to the window, from the nursery to the bedroom, even from one quarter of the town to another, and back, these little acts of motion he was in a fair way of making . . . [21]

What could be read exclusively in the reductive form of a neurotic confession and purely biographical narrative retracing psychological problems – in sum, a sort of self-portrait (which Beckett's biographers have not failed to identify as such)[22] – can also be understood as another, subtle, latent way of resolving an insoluble literary problem by way of contradiction itself. The constant toing-and-froing that characterizes Beckett's early works is not only inscribed in the geographico-literary space it depends on, but also provides for so many ways of using cunning and finding a middle way between leaving and returning, writing and remaining silent.

A Literary Atheism

Beckett was to work on a specific 'implementation' of Geulincx, notably in his first novel *Murphy*. The latent framework of the novel is an almost literal staging of the presuppositions of Geulincx's system: 'Thus Murphy felt himself split in two, a body and a mind . . . he felt his mind to be bodytight and did not understand through what channel the intercourse was effected nor how the two experiences came to overlap.'[23] Murphy's whole problem consists in imposing immobility on his body, so as to allow his mind to move in complete freedom: 'it was not until his body was appeased that he could come alive in his mind'; 'Soon his body would be quiet, soon he would be free.'[24] What has elsewhere been called 'internal exile' is to be taken literally here: Murphy seeks the redemptive exile of his soul, finally released from corporeal vicissitudes and constraints. That is why the normative discourse of psychiatry, represented at MMM ('Magdalen Mental Mercyseat') by Dr. Angus Killiecrankie, is challenged. If the task of the psychiatrist is to 'reconcile' disjoined body and mind, if the 'function of treatment is to bridge the gulf', then Murphy is radically opposed to the self-evidence of 'the rudimentary blessings of the layman's reality':

All this was duly revolting to Murphy, whose experience as a physical and rational being obliged him to call sanctuary what the psychiatrists called *exile* and to think of the patients not as banished from a system of benefits but as escaped from a colossal fiasco . . . what he called his mind functioned not as an instrument but as a place, from whose unique delights precisely those current facts *withheld* him . . .[25]

In his ironic, rigorous manner, Beckett succinctly sets out the principles of Geulincx's system in what Deleuze calls the 'great sixth chapter'.[26] The presence of this meta-discourse is clearly highlighted and almost seems to perform the role of the preambles or rules that appear in subsequent texts, giving directions for use and providing a 'reader's guide': 'It is most unfortunate, but the point of this story has been reached where a justification of the expression "Murphy's mind" has to be attempted.' And Beckett concludes: 'This painful duty having now been discharged, no further bulletins will be issued.'[27] This species of foreword supplies the quasi-totality of conceptual keys required for a clear understanding of the text and an almost literal, or at any rate faithful, resumption of Arnold Geulincx's arguments and propositions.

Playing on the difference in register between the prosaic and the speculative, contrary to the habitual loftiness of philosophy and philosophers, Beckett takes the derisory example of a kick ('[h]e neither thought a kick because he felt one nor felt a kick because he thought one').[28] Beckett accepts Geulincx's logic, which regards the 'partial congruence' of body and mind as the result of divine intervention. For him, however, this is a formal solution, since 'the problem was of little interest'. Such radical dualism conforms to his psychological disposition (or that attributed to his character by the narrator): 'Any solution would do that did not clash with the feeling, growing stronger as Murphy grew older, that his mind was a closed system, subject to no principle of change but its own.'[29]

But it also provides Beckett with a formal solution that governs the book's organization: 'Of infinitely more interest than how this came to be so was the manner in which it might be exploited.'[30] In chapter 6, where he underscores one of the major contradictions at the heart of all his future work, and which are doubtless the basis of the misunderstanding he has been subject to, Beckett reasserts his refusal of, and distaste for, the 'idealist tar'. And yet he seems to come close to a radical spiritualism: might not the absolute primacy of mind over body expounded in *Murphy*, which Beckett even seems to want to illustrate through literature, be construed as affirming an absolute idealism? On the contrary, Beckett adheres to a dualism that allots equal space to both orders, the material and the spiritual ('[t]here was the mental fact and there was the physical fact, equally real if not equally pleasant').[31] Beckett does not transform the freedom permitted by the 'world of the mind' into a metaphysical, romantic belief (that he leaves to Yeatsian poets). In a manifestly highly conscious fashion, he never uses the word 'soul' connected with religious, philosophical, poetic and even national vocabulary, but the rationalist term 'mind'. In this way, he effects a kind of materialization of the spiritualist problematic, rendering it prosaic: the reference to psychiatry, for example, is a way of making things of the spirit trivial and banal. Just as Freud could speak of 'psychical reality',

Beckett strips the spiritualist position of its aura, converting it into a paradoxical materialism. From this we can deduce all his distrust of poetic 'depths', his hatred of pomp, his refusal of the reality-effect in literature. The literary transmutation to which Beckett subjects philosophy is thus a prosaic metamorphosis, a kind of novelistic secularization, restoring to abstract, elevated speculations their quotidian banality. For philosophical fervour and poetic grandiloquence, for the spiritual elevation constitutive of the literary and philosophical religion, Beckett substituted an artistic atheism that even refused the postulates of representation. He rejected anything that reproduced belief in a literary beyond. The romantic tradition in literature is connected with this presupposition, which today is still largely constitutive of the poetic posture – the very thing Beckett was to wage a lifelong war on that has remained widely misunderstood. The only thing devotees of literature – those against whom he partly fashioned himself – wish to retain of him is the assertion of an exclusive idealism. But they do not appreciate that he was attempting a material reformation of the very gesture of literature.

At all events, the thought of Geulincx is what enabled him in *Murphy* to articulate his psychological stance (pessimism, even despair) with his literary project as a whole. Beckett worked on this first novelistic project between 1934 and 1937; forty-two publishers rejected it in the space of two years; and it was finally published by Routledge in London in 1938, when he had decided to settle in Paris for good. He dedicated to one of those publishers, called Doran, a small, furious oxymoronic poem:

> Oh Double Day Doran
> Less Oxy than moron
> You've a mind like a whore on
> The way to Bunderan.[32]

The Geulincxian theme combined with the Dantesque motif was the object of countless reprises and variations throughout Beckett's oeuvre. In his play *Eleutheria* (1947) we encounter a trace of this tragic quest for freedom: its hero cannot but renounce being free and will return to his bed-cage, 'his scrawny back turned on mankind'.[33] The divorce between the mental and physical orders is ubiquitous in *Molloy* (1948): 'And when I see my hands, on the sheet, which they love to floccillate already, they are not mine, less than ever mine, I have no arms, they are a couple, they play with the sheet, love-play perhaps, trying to get up perhaps, one on top of the other.'[34] Even the stylistic concerns bound up with the use of tenses are over-determined by an identification with Geulincx's principles. Indeed, just as the separation of body and soul involves a disjunction between movement and will, so the temporal continuity between present and future is rendered problematic, since it is deferred to God's intervention. In Beckett the refusal to exit from the exclusive self-evidence of the present and project oneself into a hypothetical future takes the specific, stylistic form of a dread of the future. 'And here I am forced into various futures,' he wrote in the short story *Le calmant*, composed at the same time.[35]

'La fin': Self-Portrait as a Family Idiot

Immediately after the war, in 1946, Beckett wrote a short story in French that was initially entitled 'Suite' and then 'La fin', part of which appeared in the July 1946 issue of *Les Temps Modernes*. It very precisely marks the joint between the texts of the 'beginning' and those of the 'end'.

In an intellectual idealization of the tinker,[36] the short story evokes what Beckett might or would like to have been, had he not left Dublin for Paris and re-dedicated himself to writing: the urge to give up, to be alien to everything, to all the world's injunctions, for want of being present in it in any way; which would have been the end of a writer so driven to renunciation that he would have preferred the Geulincxian solution of the total foreignness of mind and body, their incorrigible separation, to any engagement, always defeated in advance, in the world. The mysterious last sentence of the narrative changes the whole perspective of the writing: 'The memory came faint and cold of the story I have told, a story in the likeness of my life, I mean without the courage to end or the strength to go on.'[37] The narrator dies thinking about the story that he might have fashioned of his life; and the author pushes realism to the point of confusing the death of the narrator with the disappearance (or non-existence) of the text.

The short story can be read as one of Beckett's most exhaustive attempts to describe all the 'practical' implications of Geulincx's principles. 'The End' is the story of a quest for immobility and serenity, the story of someone 'becoming Belacqua' in order to attain freedom. Ejected from a hospital or asylum, the narrator, who recounts his life in the first person, finds a room for rent in a basement and only asks to remain immobile, to see and hear as little as possible of the world. However, divested of his money, he wanders here and there, sleeps on a dung heap, is expelled from everywhere, circulates through town and countryside, and then finds refuge in a cave at the sea's edge, where a man he knows takes care of him: 'I lay in the cave and sometimes looked out at the horizon.'[38] He then gets to a cabin in the mountains, a ruin without doors or windows, before coming back down into the town where he 'begged at a sunny corner',[39] and ends up under an overturned small boat in a garden. The narrator gradually divests himself, gives up his money, his clothing, and human company: 'That no one came any more, that no one could come any more to ask me if I was all right and needed nothing, distressed me then but little.'[40] He becomes immobile and then lies down altogether. The exhaustion of the whole possible series of places, itemized one after the other – town, country, sea, mountain – and which are going to arrive on the final page to 'crush[. . .] me in a mighty systole',[41] is another way of underscoring indifference to the world: 'Normally I didn't see a great deal. I didn't hear a great deal either. I didn't pay any attention. Strictly speaking I wasn't there. Strictly speaking I believe I've never been anywhere.'[42]

The tramp encounters his absolute antithesis in the person of a 'revolutionary', who preaches Marxist (and national?) theses:

It was a man perched on the roof of a car and haranguing the passersby. That at least was my interpretation. He was bellowing so loud that snatches of his discourse reached my ears. Union . . . brothers . . . Marx . . . capital . . . bread and butter . . . lover . . . All of a sudden he turned and pointed at me, as at an exhibit. Look at this down and out, he vociferated, this leftover . . . Old, lousy, rotten, ripe for the muckheap . . . Do you hear me, you crucified bastard! cried the orator. Then I went away, although it was still light.[43]

Beckett's beggar has all the attributes of what Marx called the lumpen proletariat – those whose conditions of existence are so precarious that they cannot be redeemed by any revolutionary movement. All of Beckett's mordancy about the 'workers' only fully makes sense in this fundamental opposition to the political instance (necessarily nationalist in the Irish context): 'To beg with your hands in your pockets makes a bad impression, it irritates the workers, especially in winter. As for holding out my hand, that was quite out of the question.' He therefore gets 'a kind of board or tray and tie[s] it to my neck and waist'.[44]

Berkeley, or Irish Idealism

Enthusiastically taken up by the young Beckett, whose tutor at Trinity College, Arthur A. Luce, was the future editor of the philosopher's oeuvre, the work of George Berkeley, or the starting-point of his intellectual project at least, might be described as an attempt to transform his Irish origins (and hence his marginality) into an intellectual opposition to English omnipotence. Berkeley developed a sort of idealist war machine that challenged all the Anglo-Saxon positivism of his time.[45]

The numerous references to Berkeley's most famous saying – *esse est percipi* (to be is to be perceived) – convey an idea of Beckett's quasi-existential use of this assertion. As in the case of Geulincx, rather than making it a tool of intellectual analysis, he used it to express his indifference to the world. Berkeley's idealism complements Geulincx's in Beckett's intellectual and illustrative arsenal of the 1930s. The idealist problematic is much in evidence in *Murphy*, in particular when the issue of existence is linked to external perception: 'Murphy began to see nothing . . . being the absence (to abuse a nice distinction) not of *percipere* but of *percipi*.'[46] Likewise, in *Watt* only perception of another renders existence necessary and hence certain.

This is a strange, literary use of philosophy. Beckett made it a kind of reservoir of references and, above all, a reassuring instrument of identification. Berkeley, an Irish (and thus for him closer) form of Geulincx's position, allowed Beckett to claim that his sceptical existential position was not merely some kind of intellectual caprice. The philosopher, who belongs to the Irish intellectual pantheon, justifies, historically as it were, his 'secular' idealism. Gilles Deleuze has underlined this kind of cultural 'kinship' between Beckett and Berkeley in his analysis of *Film*, entitled 'The Greatest Irish Film' ('the transition from one Irishman to another').[47] But he does not relate it to intellectual or aesthetic history and consequently does not precisely identify either the specific logic, or the formalist option, that Beckett derived from it. Since he ignores the writer's specifically aesthetic labour (not conceptual, despite his constant use of philosophical concepts), Deleuze believes that he can see in the final 'rocking chair' 'the Platonic idea of the Rocking Chair, the rocking chair of the spirit . . . set in motion'.[48] Yet the Geulincxian quest for ataraxy can provide an answer to the question raised by Deleuze himself at the beginning of his text: 'There must be something unbearable in the fact of being perceived, [but what?]'.[49]

In one of his interviews with Lawrence Harvey in 1962, Beckett referred to Berkeley in connection with his sense of being absent to the world, his feeling of 'existence by proxy': 'he made an association between this feeling and the idealist philosophy of Berkeley. Perhaps it was an Irish thing, basically a scepticism before nature as given, complicated by a scepticism about the perceiving subject as well.'[50] By associating the tradition of scepticism with Irishness, Beckett highlights the fact that this critical Irish attitude is constituted as a kind of historical insistence, a general mood about the world supposedly characteristic of the majority of Irish intellectuals, marked as they are by a colonial history of extreme violence. The most intellectualistic variety of scepticism would then be an expression of historical distrust of good sense and the most widely shared things in the world – a kind of problematization of the common sense that makes the order of the world utterly self-evident.

Film is to be understood in this sense. There Beckett explicitly adopts Berkeley's proposition *esse est percipi*, declaring on the first page: 'No truth value attached to above, regarded as of merely structural and dramatic convenience.' The initial hypothesis is as follows:

> All extraneous perception suppressed, animal, human, divine, self-perception maintains in being.
> Search of non-being in flight from extraneous perception breaking down in inevitability of self-perception.[51]

Taking idealist logic to the limit (and the absurd), Beckett seeks the conditions of possibility for non-existence: if *esse est percipi*, then *non esse est non percipi*. On what conditions can we not be perceived? How can we escape perception in order to accede to ataractic non-existence, the image of solitude and freedom for Geulincx? The dramatic progression of *Film* strictly respects these initial propositions: the argument exhausts all their possibilities. O – the object (Buster Keaton) – is pursued by E – the eye (the camera lens), 'the former in flight, the latter in pursuit'.[52] O can (just) escape the gaze of others (the couple) and the gaze of an animal (the monkey on the woman's shoulder). He manages to elude the camera lens, goes back to his room, closes the window, ejects dog, cat and parrot, 'approaches mirror from side, picks up rug, holding it before him, covers mirror with it again'.[53] He smashes to pieces the chromo representing God the Father and tears up photographs, but only finally to realize with horror that he cannot escape his perception of himself: 'inevitability of self-perception' prevents achievement of Geulincxian non-existence, of the 'Belacqua fantasy'.

Thus, Beckett's concern is doubtless not (as Deleuze believed) to run through 'the three great elementary images of the cinema, those of action, perception, and affection'.[54] The transformation of a technical philoso-phical proposition into a (virtually) narrative film of pursuit featuring Buster Keaton is of the same order as his attempts to undermine literary propri-eties. In ironic and formal fashion, Beckett proceeds to overturn the self-evident narrative and realist assumptions of cinema, inaugurating a new cinematographic 'genre': the speculative 'drama' and 'thriller'.

Le Dépeupleur: Depletion Depleted

Le Dépeupleur (written between 1967 and 1970) is likewise directly derived from the same problematic. With no explicit reference to Geulincx's theory or the privileged figure of Dante's Belacqua, the text remains (and intentionally so) an unfathomable enigma that appears to critics, who have suggested numerous interpretations of it,[55] 'external to any rational discourse . . . a great mystery' or even as a 'mystery that seems to surpass understanding'.[56] Tzvetan Todorov among others has proposed reading Le Dépeupleur as a rewriting of the Platonic myth of the cave; Alain Badiou suggests that it involves a sort of parable on human desire ('Beckett,' he writes, 'manages to derive criteria for classifying human multiplicity').[57] Antoinette Weber-Caflisch, who has devoted a whole work exclusively to Le Dépeupleur, rejects both the allegorical and the realist readings. She suggests referring to William Blake's drawings in order to understand Beckett's artistic approach and accepting the idea of the text's polysemy.

The strange translation of the French title in Beckett's English version – The Lost Ones – indicates that the 'depletion' in question is the gradual process that occurs in bodies. It is renunciation, the gradual separation of soul and body, desire and body, of movement, of will and body (the 'depleter' of the title is the site – the cylinder – where people are 'depleted', where bodies are emptied out). This is what in *Murphy* Beckett calls 'exile', of which he gives a definition in the novel that makes the project of *The Lost Ones* perfectly clear: 'As he lapsed in his body he felt himself coming alive in mind, set free to move among its treasures.'[58]

In this disturbing text Beckett does nor recount or 'represent' (in the sense of an allegory, for example). He uses conceptual material as a matrix of composition and a constraint on it: the conception of ataractic freedom theorized by Geulincx allows for the elaboration of a literary text that does not pertain to any recorded category. It is neither a (linear) narrative, nor a metaphor (a meaning that transcends the text). It is a species of figuration of an intellectual position, which takes the consequences of a radical idealism to their limits. Beckett proposes the literary rendition of a philosophical position that refuses embodiment, without giving credence to interiority (thus once again demonstrating his propensity for only taking up untenable positions aesthetically).

The bodies that go round and round in the 'cylinder' are categorized according to their appetite for motion, which is the only principle of division in this universe: 'Firstly those perpetually in motion. Secondly those who sometimes pause. Thirdly those who short of being driven off never stir from the coign they have won . . . Fourthly those who do not search or non-searchers'.[59] Beckett counters the common sense that identifies immobility with the properties of death and attributes positive criteria to motion. Illustrating very precisely the already cited precepts of Geulincx, who limited the principle of action (*Ubi nihil vales, ibi nihil velis* and *Quod nescis quomodo fiat, id non facis*), Beckett seeks to illustrate the logic of the paradoxical quest for freedom according to Geulincx: disinterest in the body or desertion of it, the better to ensure intellectual freedom. The bodies in motion in the cylinder are gradually emptied (depleted) of any dependence on a will that moves them. Since they cannot know (and the agitation of the searchers that gradually abates attests to it), they no longer want to will, and gradually become the 'vanquished' who have completely deserted their bodies ('[n]one looks within himself where none can be. Eyes cast down or closed signify abandonment and are confined to the vanquished').[60] Thus, in an inversion of the obvious truths of physics and metaphysics, what is 'for the best' in the cylinder is the extinction of any desire, any motion (including of the eyes), represented by the languid pose of all those bodies that have finally found their freedom. If a motion, even imperceptible, persists, it is because ataractic paradise has not yet been attained; it is because all is not yet for the best: 'But the persistence of the twofold vibration suggests that in this old abode all is not yet quite for the best.'[61] Doubtless we should also see in this collective dimension of ataractic experience a representation of wisdom according to Schopenhauer, who suggested counter-posing to the absurd power of the 'will to be' a 'negative' happiness – the extinction of any desire, abstinence and non-procreation being the only things that could ensure the suspension of pain and tranquillity in deliverance.[62]

In other words, we prevent ourselves understanding the formal and conceptual ambitions of a text as obscure as *The Lost Ones* if we simply apply common-sense notions and read it in abstraction, without relating it to the whole history of Beckett's oeuvre. Intuitive obviousness, for example, attributes to the idea of motion a positive connotation and to that of immobility (assimilated to death) a negative dimension – a topos inherited from Pascal, in particular, and his famous saying: 'Our nature consists in movement; absolute rest is death.'[63] Thus, Weber-Caflisch writes for example: 'The searcher is nothing other than the living human being, while the non-searcher is the same human being once dead.'[64] Similarly, Badiou writes that Beckett distinguishes between 'humans who search and those who have abandoned searching. The latter have given up on their desire . . . These defeated searchers are called vanquished . . . certainly, we can be vanquished – that is, defeated in the desire that constitutes us.'[65] The whole enormous historical detour that I have proposed (which passes, in particular, through Ireland) makes it possible to invert the meaning ordinarily attributed to these seemingly banal categories – motion as unhappiness and damnation, immobility as *promesse de bonheur* – and restore to this mysterious text its aesthetic and conceptual coherence.

The Lost Ones is possibly the text in which Beckett best manages to harmonize all the major 'operators' of his literary creation. The reference to Dante's *Purgatorio* is ubiquitous both as a figurative reference – Dante likewise escapes both allegory and realism, while succeeding in speaking of himself and the world; while the 'cylinder' could, following those of Dante and Joyce, be Beckett's version of Purgatory – and in the form of explicit citations. Once again, but never perhaps so fittingly, Belacqua is a perfect image of Geulincxian freedom, of virtually empty corporeality, of minimal embodiment. The posture of Belacqua as evoked by Dante is referred to twice – first in the opening pages, in a periphrastic form, to designate those who are seated 'in the attitude which wrung from Dante one of his rare wan smiles';[66] and then, right at the end, by the almost explicit reprise of the description of the character of Belacqua in *The Divine Comedy*: 'She squats against the wall with her head between her knees and her legs in her arms. The left hand clasps the right shinbone and the right the left forearm.'[67]

The recurrent theme of blindness, linked to that of perceptual existence stated by Berkeley, is also connected with the description of the 'little people' of Belacquas living in the cylinder. Non-existence, posited as the requisite end in this Geulincxian universe, takes the form of the wearing out, attenuation and then disappearance of perception, applying the inverted Berkeleyan precept that has already been cited: *non esse est non percipi*. The dessicated skin of the bodies, hampering the very action of love,[68] gradually renders any desire impossible: 'the prostration of those withered ones filled with the horror of contact and compelled to brush together without ceasing'[69] leads to the non-perception of others and retreat into solitude. Subjected to this climate, the eyes themselves become so blind that, any mode of external perception (tactile or visual) having been exhausted and each 'searcher' having been 'vanquished', the utopia of collective non-existence as proposed in *Film* can be posited as the 'end' (in all senses) of the text.[70] This blindness has likewise repeatedly been regarded as a negative element synonymous with unhappiness and fatality.

Just as the motion of bodies, ladders or eyes was opposed to any rest (to the 'stillness of the vanquished', says Beckett), to any permanent deliverance, so, in accordance with the idealist precept that the world only exists when I perceive it and ceases to exist once it is no longer perceived, the cylinder, now unperceived by the bodies, all of which have become immobile and blind – non-perceiving – also disappears. Not only light, but also variations of temperature, which inflict constant suffering on the bodies, vanish at the same time as the last of the vanquished stretches out, eager to rediscover, as in the burnt eyes of the 'aged vanquished,' the 'calm wastes' that are empty eyes, liberated from perception: 'He himself after a pause impossible to time finds at last his place and pose whereupon dark descends and at the same instant the temperature comes to rest not far from freezing point.'[71]

Thus philosophical texts become for Beckett what might be called literary 'operators'. He employs them neither philosophically – to express in literary mode a speculative vision of the world – nor in literary fashion: we should see in his texts neither metaphor nor allegory – no meaning beyond the textual surface, no message to be deciphered under the manifest appearance. The texts are written 'beyondless' and 'thenceless', as Beckett puts it in *Worstward Ho*. They merely recount the process of their begetting, or the exhaustion of the logical and formal possibilities and consequences of a proposition arbitrarily given as motor and principle of the writing. This does not mean that they do not express a particular view of the world and relationship to it (in particular, the conviction of a beneficial, necessary division between the corporeal order and the intellectual order), by means of references to philosophy. But we should not look to them for any revelations about 'man', the 'world', 'Being', 'God', or 'existence'.

The success of *Waiting for Godot* and its assimilation to the Theatre of the Absurd doubtless made a major contribution to such misunderstanding, by giving credence to the idea of a hidden meaning and an ultimate truth – an idea that still characterizes the most widespread (and utterly deadly) image of Beckett. The philosophers have latched on to his work, discovering in it a theology without God or an Existentialism, and share 'belief' in an ultimate message that it would suffice for them to decode with conceptual instruments. Given that they annex literature for philosophical purposes, ignoring the specificity of the literary phenomenon and the true novelty of Beckett's literary project, they have few chances of perceiving the reality and coherence of his oeuvre.

4

The Invention of Abstract Literature

In 1937 Beckett finally left the impossible waiting-site that was Ireland–Purgatory – a place he had not been able to settle in but not abandon either, where he mimed infernal, interminable motion; where he could neither begin nor end. His relations with his mother had gradually disintegrated and he suddenly found the courage to announce his definitive departure for Paris.

Having explored all the possibilities of the Irish literary universe and taken his place in its internal debates; having battled against Yeatsian poets and national prudery; having sought to establish himself in London as an Irish writer and supported Joyce in his subversive struggle against nationalist prejudices; but having also, and perhaps especially, sought to escape Joyce's literary and aesthetic sway, Beckett returned to Paris after seven years and decided to settle there this time. The false asylum of London had proved sterile and futile; and internal exile in Ireland, even when combined with the stoical freedom advocated by Geulincx, had not allowed him to find a true literary way out. It was not out of mere imitation of the master by the follower that he chose Paris, but because his literary, political and aesthetic stance, his general 'mood' about the world and literature, was the same – because the road mapped out by his elder seemed to him to be the most acceptable one. He opted for exile in Paris like someone who surrenders after having tried everything, but is determined to find his own way.

As soon as he arrived in Paris, he resumed contact with Joyce, who rapidly enrolled him under his banner to re-read the proofs of the first and third parts of *Work in Progress* – a task for which Joyce paid him with 250 francs, an old pullover and five ties that he wanted to get rid of. Joyce also returned to the idea realized ten years earlier with *Our Exagmination*: to publish some critical essays to get people talking about the forthcoming work. Accordingly, Joyce commissioned a new text from Beckett, which he hoped to have published in *La Nouvelle Revue Française*. Beckett initially accepted, but then abandoned the idea, even promising himself that he would never again write anything 'on command for Joyce'.[1]

Lawrence Harvey notes that the poems Beckett wrote in Paris between 1937 and 1939, his first texts in French, published after the war by Sartre in *Les Temps Modernes*,[2] were also the first to mark a pause: 'he no longer felt the need to seek, to flee, to hide. The agitation and movement, the interminable walks that recur in *Echo's Bones* are for the most part missing in these poems. Instead we find stasis.'[3] Beckett, who told Harvey that for him 'coming to Paris was like coming home',[4] finally seemed to have found somewhere he could halt and lift the curse of anxiety and perpetual motion. Some years later, we shall find in his second novel *Watt* (written in 1942 in Roussillon, where he had taken refuge to escape the Gestapo), this almost joyous, incredulous assertion of having found a place where he could stay and work – in short, finally 'endure'.

Obviously, I do not wish to reduce the early texts to transcriptions pure and simple of Beckett's actual life; and, having demonstrated their extreme subtlety in both construction and referential intricacy, I am not seeking to reduce the novellas and novels to mere illustrated discourses on Beckett himself, or banal selected passages for an autobiography. Instead, it is a question of deciphering these texts as so many attempts to define and claim the position that he intended to occupy in the Irish literary space; and to make known the aesthetic camp he was henceforth to be ranged in. By demonstrating the influence of history and the particular view of the world that derived from Beckett's specific situation in the literary universe, from which his viewpoint on that universe issued, I am seeking to show how all his work was geared to tearing himself away from that particular history, to erasing all historical traces of his individual trajectory, in order to transform them. These traces, which the literary work of the future effaced, can still be deciphered in the early writings. They must be extracted and disclosed if we are to have any chance of understanding the form and intention of his whole literary endeavour.

Up until the end of the war, nothing arrived to resolve Beckett's literary dilemma; no literary way out offered itself. Apart from *Watt*, which is a strange novelistic endeavour, abortive in many respects and unsatisfying for him, no exit seemed to present itself to him: 'It is an unsatisfactory book, written in dribs and drabs, first on the run, then of an evening after the clod-hopping, during the occupation'.[5] In 1946 he was just forty. None of the refusals of his youth – to embark on the career held out by his father, to teach at Trinity College, to find work in Ireland, to marry on his mother's instructions, to lead a 'normal' social life, to remain in Dublin, to write easy books and articles – had been rewarded, that is, converted into literature, with any success at all. *Murphy* was published in 1938 after being rejected by forty-two publishers in two years. Of the print run of 1,500, 782 unsold copies were remaindered in 1942. In *Krapp's Last Tape*, alluding to the book's failure, Beckett has Krapp say: 'Seventeen copies sold, of which eleven at trade price to free circulating libraries beyond the seas. Getting known.'[6] *Watt* did not find a publisher (it was only published nearly ten years later in 1953, in Paris in English by Olympia Press). No recognition arrived to vindicate his literary, aesthetic, political and even familial or professional choices – nothing that might really demonstrate that as an artist he had the right to an exceptional status and singular way of life.

In pre-war Paris, however, he had been part of the group around Joyce and met the writers, painters and intellectuals of Montparnasse. He now lived with the pianist Suzanne Dumesnil, whom he subsequently married, and took part in the Resistance during the war. He gradually broke his remaining links with Ireland: Joyce died in January 1941; his mother, nothing of whose he wished to keep, died in 1950.

'Plastic Meditations'

A solution was suddenly going to present itself to him, immediately after the war. Deirdre Bair recounts the scene as an almost mystical vision that Beckett supposedly had during a stay in Ireland in 1946.[7] Citing a passage from *Krapp's Last Tape* (1958), she takes the monologue literally as biography:

> Spiritually a year of profound gloom and indigence until that memorable night in March, at the end of the jetty, in the howling wind, never to be forgotten, when suddenly I saw the whole thing. The vision at last . . . What I suddenly saw then was this, that the belief I had been going on all my life . . . clear to me at last that the dark I have always struggled to keep under is in reality my most . . .

unshatterable association until my dissolution of storm and night with
the light of the understanding and the fire . . .[8]

This Beckettian 'revelation' obviously has nothing to do with Claudel's
'pillar'. But commentators like to recount it to reinforce the idea of a writer
proximate to metaphysical (if not mystical) concerns, who only set about
producing an oeuvre after having received a kind of divine grace or
inspiration. However, this was no abrupt, passive illumination. Beckett's
'vision' was at once the result of a very long process and the outline of a
practical (one might almost say 'technical') solution to an aesthetic impasse.
For him this unique moment, whose trace he wished to preserve (to the
point of inscribing it in one of his texts) – this allusive, fleeting 'turning-
point', as he wrote in another version of the text[9] – unquestionably
signalled a concrete way out of the literary aporia he was imprisoned in for
many years. The solution hit upon was so satisfying that it enabled him to
start work straight away. Accordingly, from this famous night in 1946 dates
Beckett's first great creative period, which he called 'the siege in the room'.
That year he wrote *Mercier and Camier* and *First Love* (both of them
unpublished until 1970), *The Expelled*, and *Suite* (which became *The
End*). In 1947 he began *Molloy*. In 1948 he finished *Molloy*, wrote *Malone
Dies*, and drafted *Waiting for Godot*, which he reworked and finished in
1949, before beginning *The Unnamable*.

   To explain this abrupt turnaround, the completely new creative ease that
enabled him to write the first part of his oeuvre very quickly, we must
therefore try to understand the content of his 'vision'. The only evidence
we possess as to his aesthetic and theoretical thinking at the time, which can
be regarded as a kind of 'diary' of his creation, are his texts of art criticism,
commentaries on the work of his artist friends.

   Beckett had long been interested in painting. It was McGreevy, who
became director of the National Gallery in Dublin after the war, who had
initiated him into the history of art. The great admiration of his youth was
for Jack B. Yeats, brother of the poet, from whom he would buy several
canvasses, one of which – *Morning* – was displayed everywhere he lived. In
London in 1935 he roamed galleries and museums, and was especially
interested in Dutch painting. He also knew the artistic avant-garde very
well. His six-month journey to Germany in 1936, which he described to
Harvey as a trip from one museum to the next, acquainted him with the
German output of the 1920s and 30s. He admired Kirchner, Nolde,

Heckel and had access to the finest private collections in Germany, which would enable him to see works by Picasso, Klee, Kandinsky, Mondrian, but also Cézanne, Léger, Chagall, Munch, and so forth. In Paris he met Marcel Duchamp (with whom he played chess) and Giacometti at Mary Reynolds's, but also Peggy Guggenheim, who had just opened her own gallery in London, and above all Geer and Bram Van Velde. He had made the acquaintance of the two painter brothers in 1937, shortly after he had settled for good in Paris and, from his first meetings with Peggy Guggenheim, praised the exceptional qualities of Geer Van Velde, who (according to him) merited a personal exhibition in her gallery. The exhibition occurred in 1938 in London. It did not have the success that Beckett had hoped for: critics accused Van Velde of imitating Picasso. The importance of his meeting with Bram Van Velde was so great for Beckett that in 1952, when he was beginning to become known, he wrote:

> Bram especially shouldn't think that I'm distancing myself from him: quite the reverse. The more I shut myself up, the more I feel at his side and the extent to which, despite the differences, our adventures are very similar in being insane and distressing. And should there be a [illegible] way out of it for me, I flatter myself that it would be his and no one else's. Whether people believe it or not makes no difference . . . Bram is my great familiar in work and in the impossibility of working; and that is how it will always be. [10]

This (friendly) stress on the coincidence of their 'adventures' indicates the central, analogical character of Beckett's reflections on pictures. In so far as it was 'modern' – that is, broke, particularly via abstraction, with the obvious assumptions of representation – painting became for him in the post-war years the occasion for drawing a parallel between problems in the plastic arts and literary questions. Very soon he integrated the formal questions posed by avant-garde painters into his thinking as a writer. 'There are Braques that resemble plastic meditations on the means employed,' he wrote at the time.[11] Similarly – and this is the main thing for understanding his subsequent oeuvre – there were to be Becketts that reflect on the literary means employed to continue writing while repudiating, so far as possible, representation.

While Beckett was at Saint-Lô in 1945, having just finished *Watt*, *Les Cahiers de l'Art* requested a critical essay on the painting of Bram and Geer

Van Velde, on the occasion of their respective exhibitions at the Mai and Maeght galleries. 'La Peintures des Van Velde ou Le Monde et le Pantalon', which Beckett wrote a few months before his 'vision', is an initial critical clarification, a work of commentary and explanation of the two oeuvres, but also a series of points against art criticism and common sense. Against 'representative arts', which had tried desperately 'to arrest time by representing it', the works of the Van Velde brothers 'coincide at the heart of the precise dilemma of the plastic arts: How to represent change? . . . What remains for them to represent if they renounce representing change?'.[12] 'A. Van Velde paints extension. G. Van Velde paints succession'.[13] An ironic, resolute, and deliberately obscure essay – 'unpleasant, confused chattering', says Beckett, who emphasizes modern art defined as an examination of the object of representation[14] – Le Monde et le Pantalon is also a self-portrait as an art-lover. Evoking the impotence of the critics (whom he knew from his trip to Germany) – Grohmann on Kandinsky, Sauerlandt on Ballmer, but also McGreevy on Yeats – he counter-posed to them the model of the '(enlightened) amateur', 'the harmless screwball who, in the same way that some rush to the cinema, rushes to galleries, museums and even churches in the hope – wait for it – of enjoyment . . . It's people like him that justify the existence of painting as a public phenomenon.'[15]

In 1948 – the year that saw publication of Molloy and Malone Dies – in the Maeght gallery's review, Derrière le miroir, another article appeared on the Van Velde brothers under the title 'Les peintres de l'empêchement'. Brevity possibly obliging him to be clearer and more rigorous, Beckett wrote a very beautiful text, which still surprises on account of its tone of unshakeable aesthetic certainty. Beckett takes a stand, polemicizes, and engages:

> The history of painting is the history of its relations with its object . . .
> The object of representation always resists representation . . . A first assault on the object, now grasped, independently of its qualities, in its indifference, its inertia, its latency – this is a definition of modern painting which is probably no more ridiculous than the others.

Having excluded from this definition, 'without any value judgement', the Surrealists, Mondrian and Malevich, Beckett included in it Matisse, Bonnard, Villon, Braque, Rouault and Kandinsky: 'pursuit not so much of the thing as of its thing-like character . . . what remains to be

represented if the essence of the object is to evade representation? It
remains to represent the conditions of this evasion.'[16]
   Despite his hesitation over an exercise for which he did not feel
competent ('[t]his is what is to be expected when you let yourself get
conned into writing on painting. Unless you are an art critic'), we see
emerging in this text, in Beckett's own terms, both the creative aporia and
the resolution of that aporia – the paradoxical solution that he was to
explore throughout his life, and which he here regards as making for the
greatness and vitality of the 'Paris School'. The Van Velde brothers do not
paint an object but, in a formula that has become famous, the very
'impediment' to painting objects in two different ways:

> These two kinds of artist, these two kinds of impediment – the
> object-impediment and the eye-impediment – have always existed.
> But such impediments were taken into account. There was an
> accommodation. They did not form part of representation – or
> scarcely. Here [in Bram Van Velde] they do form part of it. The
> greatest part, it might be said. What is painted is what impedes
> painting.[17]

The aesthetic and logical inversion that was to be effected in Beckett's texts
on this basis had found its initial form or formulation: in order to escape the
'I cannot paint', it is necessary to paint what impedes painting. Beckett's
thinking on writing is latent in this text: we see him operating a kind of
theoretical translation by imputing to a painter a line of thought that is not
specifically his.
   All the writers who worked with direct reference to the pictorial avant-
garde before Beckett – Apollinaire, Cendrars, Gertrude Stein, Ramon
Gomez de la Serna, and so on – count among the greatest literary
innovators of the twentieth century. Thanks to the model of painting,
they worked on the most profound problematization of narrative, figurative or poetic presuppositions. And this literary upheaval and revolution are
to be attributed to the considerable progress of painters and visual artists in
formal matters – that is, to their autonomy and freedom. In a letter of 1937
Beckett cited Gertrude Stein's 'logographs' as the enterprise closest to what
he had in mind, even if he regarded them as a failure because for him the
means prevailed over the end.[18] The need to usher literature into
modernity on the basis of the most advanced model of painting was

doubtless a constant preoccupation for him. The investigation of 'modern' solutions to dramatic dialogue, like the unprecedented use of tapes in *Krapp's Last Tape*, can be understood in this way. His radio plays, which responded to new demands for a writer; his interest in contemporary music, imparting another dimension to his texts; his acceptance of the particular constraints of television – these are so many examples of Beckett's wish to transform literature and have it attain a formal modernity that it had lacked and still did. But he came up against the retardation in the thinking of writers (especially novelists), who, outside poetry, had never yet radically challenged the principle of representation; the complete absence of accumulated techniques and forms; and the lack of an already constituted abstract literary 'syntax' and language that would rapidly enable him to find a way of his own. No doubt his lack of interest, at least in appearance, in the parallel investigations of formalist poetry is to be attributed to his hatred of 'poetic poetry' and loathing for Druidic romanticism.

At all events, his art criticism texts enabled him to continue the literary debate by other means and clarify his aesthetic positions. Realism was the main enemy (whether pictorial or literary changed nothing as to its character):

> Sweating in front of his waterfall and cursing the clouds, the 'realist' has never ceased to beguile us. But let him no longer come and bore us with his stories about objectivity and observing things. Of all the things no one has ever seen, his waterfalls are most certainly the most amazing.[19]

But his clear rejection of realist naivety did not attract him to Surrealism. Several times and on different occasions,[20] he refused the aesthetic principles of the Surrealists – that is, art as a pure product of the imagination.[21] The description of pictorial possibilities as defined by Beckett was a way of marking out the space of the aesthetic choices available to him at the end of the 1940s:

> Henceforth the painter can take one of three paths. The path of returning to the old naivety, in the twilight of its abandonment: this is the path of the penitent. Then there is a path that isn't one, but a last attempt to live on the conquered country. And finally the path *forward* of painting that is as unconcerned about an *outdated convention*

as it is about the hieratic qualities and affectations of superfluous inquiries . . .[22]

Beckett's definitive settling in Paris in this respect marked his wish to participate directly in the Parisian 'factory' of modernity. Paris had allowed Joyce a literary existence and recognition, thanks to his translation and consecration by Valery Larbaud. But it was also the meeting-place for all of modern art. In *Le Monde et le Pantalon*, defending the 'Paris School', Beckett made it the very site of artistic consecration – of the existence of artists: 'The painting of Abraham and Gerardus Van Velde is largely unknown in Paris – that is to say, it is largely unknown.'[23] Paris was the international capital of artists who refused to submit to a national vision. For Beckett, to live in the French capital and defend the art produced there was not in itself a choice in favour of France, which would repeat the nationalist assumption, but a demand for international (or anti-national) autonomy.

By showing Bram Van Velde to be the protagonist of an unprecedented break in the history of painting, Beckett also affirmed himself as a member of an artistic family or genealogy. The aesthetic investigation of painters to whom he felt close provided a support and reference-point. It was not a mere ennobling reference or term of comparison. It involved transposing the revolution of abstraction, or, more broadly, the problematization of the presuppositions of figuration, to literature. And we can better appreciate Beckett's aesthetic radicalism and desire to take the path of formal modernity in literature when we know that in 1945 his defence of Van Velde was totally anti-conformist. At the moment of their meeting in 1937, Van Velde was pursuing an oeuvre that was very different from that of the Parisian avant-garde (hence the illusion, as in the case of Beckett, of an oeuvre with no origin but itself). He was almost unknown and his exhibitions unsuccessful. This 'exceptional', 'novel' character is proof for critics today that 'his painting [was] very advanced by comparison with anything that was being done in France at the time'.[24] Beckett discovered, and sought to promote, the work of a painter who was far in advance of his time, and whose very abstraction and formalism were to help him reflect on equally radical and novel formal possibilities in literature.

In this respect the meeting between Beckett and Van Velde (born in Leiden in 1895) should be read as a mutual 'recognition'. They occupied comparable positions in Paris in more ways than one. In 1948 they were poor, unknowns, immigrants from small European countries (Van Velde spoke French badly and preferred to express himself in German – at least in the 1950s – just as Beckett continued to speak French with a strong Irish accent). They had come to Paris in search of the artistic modernity they would help to produce. They were both to pursue a radical, hermetic oeuvre in the utmost solitude.

How to Speak When Having Nothing to Say

Beckett pursued his train of thought in 1949 in the review *Transition* ('the only English-language review entirely devoted to contemporary French writing'). By now, he had already written *Molloy*, *Malone Dies* and *Waiting for Godot*; and *The Unnamable* was underway. His 'Three Dialogues' with Georges Duthuit were published in the December 1949 issue. In them Beckett expressed a deliberately iconoclastic point of view on contemporary painting.[25] He said that he preferred '[t]he expression that there is nothing to express, nothing with which to express, nothing from which to express, no power to express, no desire to express, together with the obligation to express'.[26] According to Beckett, with Bram Van Velde a new kind of art had been born. He was the first to have accepted the 'situation . . . of him who, helpless, unable to act, acts, in the event paints, since he is obliged to paint'.[27] Why, Duthuit asked, was he powerless to paint? 'Because there is nothing to paint and nothing to paint with,' Beckett replied: 'Van Velde is the first to desist from this estheticized automatism, the first to admit that to be an artist is to fail, as no other dare fail, that failure is his world'. For him it involved 'mak[ing] of submission, this admission, this fidelity to failure, a new occasion, a new term of relation, and of the act which, unable to act, obliged to act, he makes an expressive act, even if only of itself, of its impossibility, of its obligation'.[28]

In reality, this virtuoso, antinomical commentary on Van Velde allowed Beckett to address and set out the terms of the aesthetic question such as it was posed to him; and to explain how he intended to resolve the aporia confronting him. Given that he could only find a way out in the 'dark' (as he puts it in *Krapp's Last Tape*), and on condition of 'admitting' that he had to remain in this impasse in order to effect a logical reversal, he found an escape clause only in saying what prevented him from writing: expressing that there is nothing to express and that nothing can be expressed. The 'vision' summoned up by Beckett in *Krapp's Last Tape* is that of a logical (and technical) solution to an intellectual aporia, but a formal logic that is in some way 'negative', in the sense in which one speaks, for example, of negative theology: 'clear to me at last that the dark I have always struggled to keep under is in reality my most . . . unshatterable association until my dissolution of storm and night with the light of understanding and the fire'.[29] Long stuck in the brilliant Joycean dead end, Beckett was subject to the most extreme constraint and thus put on notice to think through the constraint itself. His literary enterprise could begin on the basis of an inversion of the ordinary presuppositions of literary writing: by putting the 'impediment' to painting at the heart of the artistic project, he displaced the usual aesthetic questions.

Henceforth Beckett was therefore going to try to maintain his untenable position and to stick to it for as long as possible. His daring interpretation of Van Velde was thus a kind of victory cry, the declaration of an outline solution that began to take shape for him. This doctrine of creative failure was certainly still fledgling and confused in 1949. But it was the first real practical answer that presented itself to him, in order to escape the terrible dead end he was in. For Beckett, Bram Van Velde was a painter painting the 'unpaintable', exactly as Beckett the writer was in the process of writing *The Unnamable*. In a letter to McGreevy on 13 March 1948, he writes: 'I see a little clearly at last what my writing is about and fear I have about perhaps ten years' courage and energy to get the job done. The feeling of getting oneself in perfection is a strange one, after so many years of expression in blindness.'[30]

The few indications Beckett gave Harvey are crucial in this respect. In their conversations in 1962–3, Beckett returned in virtually the same terms to his antinomic problematic: 'What complicates it all is the need to make. Like a child in mud but no mud. And no child. Only need.'[31] He even tried to find several formulations of his structurally contradictory situation: 'I write because I have to . . . What do you do when "I can't" meets "I must"? . . . Painting and music have so much better a chance.'[32] In stating what he experienced as an aporia (being at once powerless and objectless, 'without mud'), Beckett also supplied the key to his writing. Like Van Velde, he became an artist of failure, a writer who 'dared to fail' or to write only that failure – someone who produced 'an expressive act, even if only . . . of its impossibility'. The 'revelation' of winter 1946 which took shape and was moulded in these years is nothing other than that: transforming the question of failure into the very form of writing.

The practical problematic of this writing of 'impediment' has – need it be said? – nothing to do with the literary concepts of Blanchot proclaiming 'the extinction of literature' or 'the eloquent extinction of the author'.[33] Writing the 'unwritable' does not consist in postulating that literature is facing 'the test of impossibility'.[34] On the contrary, Beckett contested existential pathos and, together with the idiom of 'being', equally rejected that of the 'imaginary' or the 'total experience' of literature.[35] It was the desire to usher literature into formal modernity that enabled him gradually to abandon the presuppositions of representation and take as his object the very impediment to representing reality; or rather, to discover new literary tools to deliver a death blow to the object, whether extinct or not, and its representation. Certainly, the young Beckett's paradoxically and deliberately abstruse formulations might in part explain why he could be annexed by Heideggerian criticism, which prizes above all else the rhetoric of rhetorical paradox while claiming to repudiate rhetoric. But in refusing to 'reduce [literature] to a question of language',[36] by excluding the notion that it can be defined as 'a set of forms, or even [as] a perceptible mode of activity',[37] Blanchot prevents himself understanding Beckett's very project. Moreover, utterly misunderstood in his deliberately paradoxical and even ironic reflection, Beckett was accused by some members of the *Transition* group of wishing to make Van Velde despair and to paralyze him by having him believe that painting is an impossible act. Further still, his critical statements were later analysed in the categories established by official criticism and helped establish what long remained the only reading of Van Velde himself and of Beckett. In the case of the latter, in accordance with the classical retrospective illusion, the texts of the 1940s were read in search of the presuppositions and aesthetic of the 1960s.[38]

Beckett's statement was not reducible to a critical nihilism, but on the contrary was the motor and principle of future creation. In virtually all the interviews he gave, Beckett never stopped repeating how central formal preoccupations were for him. At the beginning of the 1960s, in his interviews with Lawrence Harvey, he denied any kinship with Surrealist 'formlessness' and asserted that he was looking for a form: 'there is a form, but it doesn't move, stand upright, have hands . . . Someone will find it someday. Perhaps I won't, but someone will.'[39] The testimony of Ludovic Janvier proceeds along the same lines: 'One will not be surprised to hear from the writer's own mouth that he was mainly preoccupied, to the point of madness, with formal beauty. This is a paradox for those witnessing what they believe to be the philosophical debate of *Waiting for Godot*'.[40] And

Tom Driver has Beckett say during their meeting in Paris: 'there will be new form . . . That is why the form itself becomes a preoccupation, because it exists as a problem separate from the material it accommodates. To find a form that accommodates the mess, that is the task of the artist now'.[41]

A Syntax of Weakness

Beckett made it clear to Harvey that his formal explorations fully shared in the 'adventure of modern art': 'Someday someone will find an adequate form, a "syntax of weakness"'.[42] With nothing to appeal to and no precedent, he was henceforth going to work on developing an abstract literary 'syntax', an equivalent of non-figurative pictorial idiom. He remained far removed from the parallel experimentation of sound poetry, for example, because he sought to 'abstractify' language — that is, to transform words into a mere material at the disposal of an abstract literary art, without reducing them to their pure sonorous materiality, without completely dissolving the specificity of language: the irreducible bond between word and thing.

To convert failure into the success of a literary project, and thereby answer the unanswerable question of 'What shall I do? What shall I do?' posed in the early pages of *Molloy*, Beckett transformed that question into the very content of writing: made the 'what to do?' the 'doing'. Via this complete inversion of the ordinary literary rules, which is in direct continuity with Joyce's literary enterprise as he had defended it in 1929, and which made the form the end of writing ('[h]is writing is not *about* something; *it is that something itself*'),[43] Beckett supplied himself with the means finally to 'commence' (*Comment c'est?*).

Proof is to be found on the first page of *The Unnamable*, exactly contemporaneous with the 'Three Dialogues', which notably evokes the issue of the aporia as something constitutive of writing or even its motor: 'What am I to do, what shall I do, what should I do, in my situation, how proceed? By aporia pure and simple? Or by affirmations and negations invalidated as uttered, or sooner or later? Generally speaking. There must be other shifts.'[44] All these questions are so many technical queries about how to construct and produce the text. The processes, the techniques of writing, the 'shifts' that Beckett lists at the beginning of his book in order to equip himself with the means to 'go on' — these represent so many rhetorical instruments (in the sense of discursive techniques) or stylistic instruments which, like Van Velde's palette, are going to allow him to invent, implement this inverted literature. Like some of Braque's canvasses according to Beckett, *The Unnamable* first of all enumerates the 'means employed' in the course of the book's unfolding. Aporia, contradiction and paradox are the initial tools (simultaneously logical and stylistic) experimented with.[45] The text applies to syntax the process predicated of contradiction ('affirmations and negations invalidated as uttered'), yielding for example:

> Having nothing to say, no words but the words of others, I have to speak . . . Not to have been a dupe, that will have been my best possession, my best deed, to have been a dupe, wishing I wasn't, thinking I wasn't, knowing I was, not being a dupe of not being a dupe . . . Labyrinthine torment that can't be grasped, or limited, or felt, or suffered, no, not even suffered . . .[46]

The major innovation of *The Unnamable* is that it made literary 'means' (rhetorical, linguistic, syntactic, metaphorical) the motor and, to a certain extent, the end of writing itself. There is no longer any 'subject' – either in the sense of painting or of philosophy – any content, and there is almost no signification either. There is only the telling of the failure to tell, just as Bram Van Velde paints the failure to paint.

Some interpreters of Beckett's oeuvre – foremost among them Ludovic Janvier, for whom 'language is indeed the subject of [Beckett's] undertaking' – have of course signalled this formalist dimension.[47] But the wish at all costs to provide a substantive, existential content, as a guarantee of 'profundity', has by the same token hampered an understanding of the complex stakes of Beckett's logic, which is laid out for the first time in all its radicalism in *The Unnamable*: 'Here all is clear. No, all is not clear. But the discourse must go on. So one invents obscurities. Rhetoric.'[48] Starting with *The Unnamable*, Beckett will provide as a preamble to each of his texts the rules governing the whole book, its unique, particular grammar and syntax. Thus, in *How It Is* (1961), he announces in the first paragraph, which very precisely sets out the content of each part, the structure of his narrative: 'how it was I quote before Pim with Pim after Pim how it is three parts I say it as I hear it'.[49] In *Company* (1985) Beckett explains his principle of construction in the first lines: 'A voice comes to one in the dark.

Imagine . . . That then is the proposition . . . Use of the second person marks the voice. That of the third that of the cantankerous other.'[50] By systematically dispelling literary beliefs, and challenging any naïve subscription on part of readers by explaining the rules and techniques of composition and the refusal of any form of realism (including the least 'reality-effect'), Beckett signals his wish to attack the very foundations of literature.

In this stubborn search for abstractive linguistic 'means', Beckett, like a painter preserving the uniqueness of each of his canvasses, and increasingly as his oeuvre developed, tried to find the maximum autonomy, starting afresh every time, for each of his texts. The principle of independence of the texts − that is, their self-generation in isolation from any external connection − is stated and justified by Beckett on the basis exclusively of the logic of the 'head'. From the adoption of the first person in the texts of the late 1940s ('All these Murphys, Molloys and Malones do not fool me. They have made me waste my time, suffer for nothing, speak of them when . . . I should have spoken of me and of me alone . . . It is now I shall speak of me, for the first time'),[51] he will write only what is 'in the head'. None of this bears the slightest resemblance to an autobiography or confession. It is simply the avowal of a writing that refuses the imperatives of realism in order to mark out memories, voices from the past, childhood, shades of mother and father, images come to haunt the memory. All the intellectual mechanisms of the internal organization and exhaustion of a proposition also find their place; and the abstract image and shadow of a memory are the material of these texts, for which the category of 'fiction' is no longer apposite. These more or less figurative 'images' structure what are virtually abstract stories, in which, decreasingly but indelibly, at least the head that fashions the image survives: 'it's done I've had the image'.[52] On the model of the freedom wrested by painters, Beckett works to invent literary images freed from figurative norms and prescriptions, including the intuitive obviousness of psychological interiority. The autonomy of each text is a kind of reiterated manifesto against the foundations of what had hitherto been regarded as constitutive of the literary (or at least of literary narrative), and which Beckett's whole oeuvre shows to be nothing but the stamp of the profound conservatism of literature, incapable of ridding itself of the presuppositions of realism.

Starting with *How It Is*, and then *Imagination Dead Imagine* (1965),

Enough and *Bing* (1966), and *Lessness* (1969), Beckett attacks the 'out-dated conventions' of literature on all fronts. He progressively jettisons from his texts all external elements that might still attach them to the literary tradition. From *The Unnamable*, which (as is clear) is a founding text for many reasons, he explicitly challenges temporal and spatial categories, historically posited as conditions of possibility of literary creation and as bases of the 'reality-effect'. The first words of the text, construed by critics (Blanchot first of all) as philosophical questions, are in fact technical questions – a way of challenging the habitual preliminaries of ordinary literature that are place, time and action embodied by characters: 'Where now? Who now? When now? Unquestioning.' A little further on, Beckett decides to suppress these conventions.

The refusal of metaphor[53] or allegory, clearly announced at the end of *Watt* ('no symbols where none intended'), will be yet another stylistic way of marking a break with the instruments of literary realism and identifying the 'adventure of modern art' with 'eliminating the artificial forms and techniques'.[54] This elimination will take the form of the progressive disappearance of characters, but also of virtually complete abolition of punctuation, setting, narrative time, narration itself, and so forth. Contrary to a spiritualist reading of Beckett's enterprise, the progressive invention of a materialist literature fashioning its own tools was also gradually to dictate the dissolution of the 'subjects' of writing in all their forms – first name and then pronoun, last trace of the presence of the narrator in the form of this 'putain de première personne'. Each text is the occasion for a new attempt, a new renunciation of literary assump-tions. Only in the 1960s, in *Bing* but especially *Lessness*, would Beckett succeed in completely erasing the subjective convention by deleting pronouns – and not in aid of a putative 'extinction of the author', but in the name of a refusal to reproduce the obviousness of psychological interiority.

The reiterated presence of the 'head' as an image factory is another way of challenging what has been constituted as the quintessential instrument of artistic creation: the imagination, or what the most conservative literary tradition also calls inspiration. This manifest refusal is a further index of Beckett's wish to contest with literary weapons the sway of philosophies of the subject, which in literature have imposed the illusion of the omni-potence of subjectivity, interiority and consciousness, and all the conse-quent prophetic representations: profundity, imagination and singularity.

Beckett vigorously reasserts this position, for example, in *Imagination Dead Imagine* (1965), whose title is virtually a manifesto in itself. 'The cranium has a monopoly on this article,' he asserted in connection with Van Velde's images,[55] thus making the provocative choice of the most objectivist (and disenchanted) version of brain functions, as opposed to the eternal grandiloquence of the 'soul'. Throughout his oeuvre we find similar materialist professions of faith. In *Nouvelles et Textes pour rien* (1950), he offers a more radical version of what he still called 'mind' in *Murphy*, by adopting the word 'head'. And in *Worstward Ho* (1983) we find '[h]ead sunk on crippled hands . . . Seat of all. Germ of all',[56] which will be objectified still further by its metamorphosis into a 'skull' and 'some soft of mind'. The persistence of a conception of thought and creation so contrary to the whole enchanted representation of creative and artistic activity that it is almost self-destructive of it, is also an act of supreme courage by an artist exhibiting not the end of art, but his wish to put an end to habitual artistic illusion and belief. The refusal of a spiritual transcendence in favour of objectively describable material functions explains how Beckett could see in the images produced by Van Velde an 'incredible objectivity'.[57]

Literature of the 'Unword'

The final obstacle to the development of the abstract literature that Beckett applied himself to, and which is also the foundation of traditional literature, is nothing other than the word. For him it was not a question of reassessing words – he did not seek to restore 'a purer meaning to the "words of the tribe"', in the words of Mallarmé; or of simply employing them 'wisely', like a good craftsman who only uses quality materials; or even – as some poets have attempted – of converting the word into pure sound freed of meaning. Instead, the issue is the celebrated correspondence, even if arbitrary, between word and thing, the inevitable existence of a signified and a referent. To proceed in the direction of 'nothing' and persevere on the path of failure as the only possible access to literary abstraction, Beckett had to invent new uses both of words and syntax, manufacture a literary material that was in some way novel, making it possible to escape signification – that is, narration, representation, succession, description, setting, and even character, without thereby resigning himself to inarticulacy.[58]

To silence meaning as far as possible, in order to accede to literary autonomy, was Beckett's wager – one of the most ambitious and radical in literary history. In a letter, addressed in German to Axel Kaun who had asked him to translate some poems by Joachim Ringelnatz into English, Beckett had at the end of the 1930s set out the thinking, fledgling but central, that was to guide his whole future enterprise:[59]

> Let us hope the time will come, thank God that in certain circles it has already come, when language is most efficiently used where it is being most efficiently misused. As we cannot eliminate language all at once, we should at least leave nothing undone that might contribute to its falling into disrepute.

According to Beckett, disrepute – that is, the end of credence in language – was the precondition for a literary revolution:

> I cannot imagine a higher goal for a writer today. Or is literature alone to remain behind in the lazy old ways that have been so long ago abandoned by music and painting? Is there something paralysingly holy in the vicious nature of the word that is not found in the elements of the other arts? Is there any reason why that terrible materiality of the word surface should not be capable of being dissolved, like for example the sound surface, torn by enormous pauses, of Beethoven's seventh symphony . . . ?[60]

Measured against the freedom and modernity of music and painting, literature's retardation was, as we can see, directly associated with the nature of the specifically literary material: the word. The enterprise of 'dissolving' the word, which Beckett says he wants to apply himself to, took the form of a radical inversion of literary imperatives. We see at work the contradiction that informed him and compelled him to assert his difference from Joyce's enterprise, while proclaiming his kinship:

> With such a program, in my opinion, the latest work of Joyce has nothing whatever to do. There it seems to be rather a matter of an apotheosis of the word. Unless pure Ascension to Heaven and Descent to Hell are somehow one and the same. How beautiful it would be to be able to believe that that was indeed the case.[61]

The dissolution of the word that Beckett says he wishes to accomplish would only be the other side, the symmetrical figure in a sense, of the 'apotheosis of the word' practised by Joyce in *Finnegans Wake*. With this simple, brilliant formula Beckett encapsulates the nature of the opposition between the two oeuvres and solves the mystery of the bond uniting them. On several occasions in interviews, but always in an allusive fashion, he stated that his project was at once the inverse of Joyce's (just as ignorance is the inverse of omniscience) and yet linked to it by its very form, symmetrically.

Beckett continued:

> On the way to this literature of the unword, which is so desirable to me, some form of nominalist irony might be a necessary stage. But it is not enough for the game to lose some of its sacred seriousness. It should stop. Let us therefore act like that mad [?] mathematician who used a different principle of measurement at each stage of his calculation. An assault against words in the name of beauty.[62]

The literature that Beckett seeks to bring into play is therefore the inverse of the poetic aestheticism persuaded of the 'beauty' of words. On the contrary, he wishes to proceed to an 'assault against words', in order to invert literature's naive relationship with language: instrumental (realism) or aestheticizing (poetry). We can read his attempt at a description of a pot in *Watt* as an echo of the 'nominalist irony' referred to in his letter of 1937:

> It resembled a pot, it was almost a pot, but it was not a pot of which one could say, Pot, pot, and be comforted. It was in vain that it answered, with unexceptionable adequacy, all the purposes, and performed all the offices, of a pot, it was not a pot. And it was just this hairbreadth departure from the true nature of a pot that so excruciated Watt.[63]

We will often find this desire to rupture the obviousness of the meaning of words flaunted, particularly in *Molloy*: 'Yes, the words I heard, and heard distinctly, having quite a sensitive ear, were heard a first time, then a second, and often even a third, as pure sounds, free of all meaning'.[64]

The absolute autonomy of every text, posited each time as an equation to be solved, also assumes an incessant labour of accumulation and reprise of earlier solutions and advances. Beckett proceeds by successive breaks, but also by an immense totalization of the most successful processes, experiments, and failures attempted in each of his texts, including the oldest ones, in order to arrive at a progressive, systematic pruning of his language.

Because Beckett was in search of a form, by definition unfinished and hypothetical, which could resolve the aesthetic and literary contradiction he had had to struggle with all his life, he proceeded by sketches that were forever being restarted, by the progressive adjustment of finds, ideas, approximations to themes and words.[65] The development of his work, the breaks and changes of tone and form, has no principle other than this constant movement required of him by the search for an 'adequate form'.

Doubtless this might partially explain his great reluctance to publish (and comment on) his early works. The writings preceding 'the siege in the room' held hardly any interest for him from the 1950s onwards, since they fell short of solving (even in part) his equation.[66] Nothing was the same, '[n]ot with the fire in me now' says Krapp at the end of *Krapp's Last Tape*. We know of Beckett's reservations about his first play, *Waiting for Godot*, and his irritation at the recognition it received throughout the world. He stated on several occasions that *Godot* was a 'bad play',[67] as if it was in some way 'obsolete' for him and its recognition simply the result of a misunderstanding that obscured his real literary enterprise.

The Unnamable is both directly continuous with everything he had attempted up until then, from the oxymorons of *More Pricks than Kicks* and the Geulincxian stance of *Murphy* to the musings of *Molloy*. And yet it broke new ground by radicalizing the earlier endeavours. Beckett reused them to different ends by combining them in almost cumulative fashion. His compositional labour should therefore not be conceived as the fulfilment of a project successfully completed and mastered in advance, but rather as a major work-site, an always unfinished quest (perhaps on the model of Joyce's *Work in Progress*), as the 'impression of hypothesis' that he discovered in certain of Braque's paintings.[68]

Thus, Beckett gradually made the transition from the idea of paradox and aporia to that of 'nothing' – Ludovic Janvier remarks of *Texts for Nothing* (completed in 1950) that they 'are not for nothing, but have nothing as their subject'[69] – and then to the idea of generalized pejoration that would reach fulfilment very late, in the 1980s, with *Worstward Ho*, the discovery of 'lessness' leading him to the logical self-evidence and consequences of subtraction. Aligning this novel grammar and its object required the examination of darkness, nothing, lessness, the nothing-to-be-said. Knowing that there was nothing to be said but nothing, a 'syntax of weakness' was the instrument with which Beckett was best (hence least) able to say what he had to say, contrary to the literary realism that believes (as did Joyce) in words and their correspondence to reality. 'Joyce believed in words,' Beckett explained; 'All you had to do was rearrange them and they would express what you wanted.'[70] Beckett sought (and found) the weakest form, the most 'zero' (in the sense in which it is said of a sum), the closest to expressing nothing, the most paradoxically adequate. He should be taken at his word when he remarked to Lawrence Harvey that 'if he were a critic setting out to write on the works of Beckett (and he thanked heaven he was not), he would start with two quotations, one by Geulincx: "Ubi nihil vales, ibi nihil velis," and one by Democritus: "Nothing is more real than nothing." '[71]

That is why a formalist, systematic reading, by accounting for the principle behind the construction of seemingly random, esoteric texts, also has the effect of dispelling their 'disturbing strangeness'. The suffering, despair or cruelty that are often regarded as constitutive of Beckett's writing fade once we understand their origin and logic. Furthermore, as Beckett seeks to put an end to the illusion of identification and psychological presuppositions that ground literary attachment, these moral categories, which readers invest in the text solely on account of the psychologizing habits instilled by the usual cult of literature, tend to disappear in favour of the aesthetic pleasure afforded by a formal exercise at once virtuoso and deeply consistent. His famous quarrels with actors or directors of his plays derived from this radical wish to eradicate the pathos of the theatrical mechanism. The systematic, avowed 'de-psychologization' of instances of dialogue, which Beckett wanted to render rhythmical and musical, was obviously opposed to any species of empathic 'interpretation' and 'identification' by the actor with the character.

French, or 'The Right Weakening Effect'

Obviously, this formal project must be related to the decision to write in French and the systematization of bilingualism that also occurred in the late 1940s and early 1950s.

Beckett's explicit desire to turn his back on Joyce's aesthetic, while always continuing to express his admiration for him, largely explains why critics, fixing on the extravagance of the one and reserve of the other, have been prevented from making much progress in relating the two oeuvres to one another. The abandonment, at least intermittently, of the English language and transformation of Beckett into a (virtually) French writer were also bound up with his difficult, conflict-ridden, and yet constitutive relationship with Ireland, his anger at the English and the Irish – an anger shared, obviously, with Joyce – and the polyglottic model of *Finnegans Wake*. In *The Unnamable* the narrator evokes (possibly for the last time in explicit fashion) 'the island':

> I'll try and look as if I was telling it willingly, to keep them quiet in case they should feel like refreshing my memory, on the subject of my behaviour above in the island, among my compatriots, con-temporaries, coreligionists and companions in distress . . . It's a poor trick that consists in ramming a set of words down your gullet on the principle that you can't bring them up without being branded as belonging to their breed. But I'll fix their gibberish for them.[72]

In other words, we cannot understand the full implications of Beckett's option for bilingualism unless we take into account all the debates peculiar to Ireland, the violent relations with England, Yeats's choice of English, Joyce's polyglottic solutions (for which Beckett himself furnished the rationale in 1929 in *Our Exagmination*), and the literary dead end Beckett found himself in. Because criticism usually rejects the idea of resituating a literary work within history, decreed external *a priori*, out of a belief in the purity of literature, it prevents itself seeing that the whole literary space is always present, in and through the set of forces it puts in place, in each choice made by a writer.

In 1937 Beckett wrote:

> It is indeed becoming more and more difficult, even senseless, for me to write an official English. And more and more my own language appears to me like a veil that must be torn apart in order to get at the things (or the Nothingness) behind it. Grammar and style. To me they seem to have become as irrelevant as a Victorian bathing suit or the imperturbability of a true gentleman. A mask.[73]

Through the play of comparisons which makes language a symbol of British propriety and prudery, we see that Beckett followed the road of subversion mapped out by Joyce. Their enterprises take the form of the same problematization of the norms of the English language and of respect for national and grammatical propriety. Starting out from these premises, however, Beckett sought a path that was peculiar to him. He responded countless times to the question of bilingualism. Harvey recounts him stating that for him as an Irishman, French represented '*a form of weakness*' compared with his mother tongue; and moreover that by contrast with the 'relative asceticism of French', English, on account of its very great richness, contained within it 'the temptation to rhetoric and virtuosity', which were 'merely words mirroring themselves complacently, Narcissus-like'.[74] To another interlocutor, he offered an even more illuminating formula, telling Herbert Blau that French attracted him because it had 'the right weakening effect'.[75]

The recurrence of the theme of weakness prompts the thought that adopting French was the first step in Beckett's option for failure and move towards 'nothing'. In his search for an 'adequate form' and 'syntax of weakness', French supplied him with a supplementary 'weakness' – the precise 'weakening effect' required to institute his aesthetic of 'nothing'. It had the advantage of serving his project to the full – of allowing him to write without effects, without rhetoric, 'without style', as he put it in 1957 to Nicholas Gessner.[76] Over and above the fact that it was obviously required of a writer seeking to become known in Paris, French was better suited to the project of Beckett, who had in mind (as he had written in *Dream of Fair to Middling Women*) the style of Racine or Malherbe: 'They have no style, they write without style, do they not, they give you the phrase, the sparkle, the precious margaret. Perhaps only the French can do it. Perhaps only the French language can give you the thing you want.'[77] Writing in French, with all the difficulty that involved, led Beckett onto the path of asceticism, prevented him from succumbing to stylistic excess, compelled him to deny himself the bouts of erudition and rhetorical virtuosity that marked all his early texts.

Beckett was to practise a well-nigh complete literary bilingualism, since he translated or rewrote almost all his texts in two languages (from French into English as well as English into French). This constant toing-and-froing between two major literary languages represents the most extreme of all the solutions adopted by writers in a situation of domination and/or exile, who (like Cioran, Nabokov or Soyinka) must often abandon their mother tongue to have any chance of a literary existence.

What is more, the division of labour Beckett assigned the two languages is itself significant. Apart from his first plays, *En attendant Godot*, which had to be presented in French to have any chance of being accepted by a Parisian theatre, and *Fin de partie*, which was dedicated to Roger Blin (but produced in London in French in 1957) and continued their theatrical collaboration, all of Beckett's dramatic pieces were initially written in English,[78] and only subsequently translated into French for the most part: *All That Fall* (1956); *Krapp's Last Tape* (1958); *Embers* (1959); *Words and Music* (1959); *Happy Days* (1961); *Play* (1963); *Come and Go* (1965); *Eh! Joe* (1965); *Breath* (1969); *That Time* (1974); *Ghost Trio* (1975); *Footfalls* (1975); *But the Clouds* (1976); *Radio I and II* (1976); *A Piece of Monologue* (1980); *Ohio Impromptu* (1981); *Rockaby* (1981); *Quad* (1981); and *What Where* (1983).[79]

We can thus venture the hypothesis that, in the early years of his literary work at least, Beckett took two distinct roads which only gradually met: on the one hand, a radical, difficult move towards a minimalist aesthetic requiring the use of French – the privileged form (according to Beckett) of a literary abstraction; on the other, development of a dramaturgy that was certainly subversive, but which remained on the figurative road, respecting the major dramatic conventions (characters, scenery, articulated text, and so forth), even when reduced to a minimum, and consequently requiring less 'weakness' and capable of bearing the 'richness' of English. Deirdre Bair relates that Beckett explained his transition to writing for the theatre with reference to a 'diversion', 'a marvellous, liberating diversion': 'I began to write Godot as a relaxation, to get away from the awful prose I was writing at the time.'[80]

From his own testimony, we also know that *The Unnamable* (written in 1949) and then *Texts for Nothing* (1950) were for him a formal dead end, terminating five years of intense creation. After composing his most ground-breaking texts, Beckett spent nearly ten years unable to take this road again. It was as if for him the trilogy (*Molloy*, *Malone Dies* and especially *The Unnamable*) had, by virtue of its radical character, attained the limits that could be accorded to the autonomy of the literary object. He wrote to McGreevy: 'I feel more and more that I shall perhaps never be able to write anything else . . . I can't go on and I can't go back. Perhaps another play someday.'[81] Up until 1960, when he wrote *How It Is*, he was unable to write anything along the same lines, confining himself to the theatre or translating earlier works. The fact that Beckett took this 'break',[82] a kind of median solution (confirmed by his almost immediate world-wide success), in the English language, supplies additional evidence of the formal use he assigned French. He used it *a contrario*, as a sort of linguistic material better suited to his search for a 'syntax of weakness'.[83]

However, in the course of his very slow development of an autonomous literary system, plays and stories gradually coincided, found common forms and processes. While painting served as a model for his exploration of narration and narrative, music, symmetrically, was probably his aid in constructing his dramatic project. In the same way that he deconstructed all the limits assigned the novel, Beckett worked to challenge the imperatives and presuppositions of theatrical representation. In his use of theatre conceived as 'an investigation of its nature',[84] he employed music as a kind of formal model, as has been attested by various actors who worked with him on productions of his plays.[85] To Ludovic Janvier he explained: 'Directors don't seem to be sensitive to *form in motion*. The kind of form you find in music, for example, where themes are reprised.'[86] Roger Blin very specifically relates his disagreements with Beckett during the production of *Endgame* (1957) to this view of forms and rhythm: 'I've the feeling that Beckett saw *Endgame* as a Mondrian painting, with very clear compartments, geometrical separations, *musical geometry*. And I somewhat rebelled against this during rehearsals, which provoked some impassioned discussions between Beckett and me.'[87]

Edith Fournier has referred to the collaboration of Beckett and the composer Marcel Mihalovici in 1961, when the latter was writing the opera *Krapp*, based on *Krapp's Last Tape*.[88] Beckett, who had a sound musical training, followed the development of the work, even proposing modifications of the score, as if music allowed him to impart an acoustic, rhythmic harmony to his text. He would fairly rapidly abandon the idea of a musical structure accompanying the organization of his words, working instead on the development of a semantic and syntactic rhythm produced by the text itself, which would be one of the ways of acceding to absolute autonomy, to literary abstraction. Written in English for television in 1980, *Quad*, a 'piece for four players, light and percussion', is perhaps the purest theatrical combinatory ever attempted, the paths of four silhouettes in 'unbroken movement': 'No colour, all four in identical white gowns, no percussion, footsteps only sound, slow tempo,' Beckett specified.[89] This pure, rhythmic abstraction literally applies his definition of theatre as 'form in motion' and, in the sphere of drama, perhaps represents the same formal result as *Worstward Ho*, written in English, in that of 'narrative'. It is as if for this text of his last years he had finally discovered in the English language, via a syntax and semantic construction that were likewise renewed, a formal, combinatory economy as effective as that previously attributed to French; or rather, as if he was using properties previously attributed to French in order to reinvent English in a new, 'weakened' form.

Order and Beauty

This new geometrical, literary syntax was also found in mathematics and logic by Beckett, who progressively arranged his texts as a type of stylistic equation. An unpublished letter to Georges Duthuit dating from 1948 helps us to understand the precise link that Beckett made between art and mathematics, which for him represented the highest degree of formal sophistication. Contrary to the commonplace view, painting, perhaps even more than music – which was nevertheless often compared to mathematics – enabled him to address the theme of the beauty of order:

> I remember a painting at the Zwinger, a Saint Sebastian by Antonello da Messina – incredible, incredible. It was in the first room; it brought me to a standstill every time. A space that was pure by virtue of being mathematical – black-and-white tiles, or rather concrete slabs, in long foreshortened figures to draw moans from you . . . and all that invaded, eaten by the human. Confronted with such a work, such a victory over the reality of disorder, pettiness of heart and mind, you fail to hang yourself.[90]

Art is a victory of order over 'the reality of disorder'. The mathematical organization of da Messina's black and white slabs, the rigorously constructed architecture, far from detracting from artistic invention and beauty, as the romantic representation of inspired disorder and frenzied genius would have it, is the result of a harmonious purity. For Beckett the abstraction and rigour of mathematics are not the antithesis of artistic inspiration, but its organizing principle. The logic consequently applied to literary objects enabled him to define a new, autonomous syntax freeing literary language from the automatic reflexes of ordinary language, to trace the contours of hitherto unknown literary forms.

Starting with the composition of *Watt*, the combinatory of semantic, syllabic, syntactic or narrative elements, the art of combining solutions, outcomes, possible responses and 'logics' to a derisory question, is a principle of internal organization of the texts and one of the sources of Beckett's irony. Initially, it involved parodic attempts to find a content for an empty plot: 'Then he took it into his head to invert, no longer the order of the words in the sentence, nor that of the letters in the word, nor that of the sentences in the period, nor that of the letters in the word . . .', and so forth.[91] After 1946 he returned, albeit less systematically, to applying a combinatory to texts, but this time with the increasingly precise project – with the help of the model of the game of chess (and perhaps also because of the word *échecs* [failures/chess] in French) – of formally exhausting a proposition. In this respect, the famous episode of the 'sucking-stones' in *Molloy* is a model of narrative logic applied to a concrete object without any significance, where nothing is at stake:

> I distributed them equally between my four pockets, and sucked them turn and turn about. This raised a problem which I first solved in the following way. I had say sixteen stones, four in each of my four pockets these being the two pockets of my trousers and the two pockets of my greatcoat. Taking a stone from the right pocket of my greatcoat, and putting it in my mouth, I replaced it [etc.] . . .[92]

From this point of view, Edith Fournier has brilliantly described the structure of *Sans* (translated by Beckett into English as *Lessness* in 1970), showing that the text is composed of two strictly equal parts of 60 sentences each, the second of which repeats the first but in a different syntactic order and in accordance with a rigorous schema and a strict distributional organization.[93]

One of the only direct 'confessions' we possess as to this logical compulsion was offered by Beckett in *Enough* (1966), which bears too close a resemblance to various childhood memories and a precise evocation of walks with his father for us to fail to take literally the final sentence ('Enough my old breast feels his hand'), which obeys the quasi-systematic principle of 'ambiguating' the narrative:

> All I know comes from him. I won't repeat this apropos of all my bits of knowledge. The art of combining is not my fault. It's a curse from above. From the rest I would suggest not guilty . . . We took flight in

arithmetic. What mental calculations bent double hand in hand. Whole ternary numbers we raised in this way to the third power sometimes in downpours of rain. Graving themselves in his memory as best they could the ensuring cubes accumulated. In view of the converse operation at a later stage.[94]

Preceding what Ludovic Janvier calls the 'deluge of logic', this confession is echoed by a statement in *How It Is*: 'I always loved arithmetic it has paid me back in full.'[95]

This form of reasoning applied to the most incongruous things – that is, objects like artistic phenomena, which usually only bear sensory evocation – is a further feature acknowledged by Beckett in connection with his text on Van Velde's painting. In 1957, when the Michel-Warren gallery organized a second exhibition by the Dutch painter, there was a plan to use the text of the 'Three Dialogues' for the invitation card. Beckett resisted, arguing that it would only do his friend a disservice. Rather than accept the philosophical interpretation of this text, diffused in the name of literary 'profundity', he wrote: 'You can't offer this dialogue for Bram's exhibition. It's *circus algebra*.'[96]

A 'space that is pure by virtue of being mathematical' is also the motor of what I call 'abstractification', in order to express both the process of enactment and implementation of a formal abstraction (which does not exclude the presence of images, but does challenge realist principles of representation), but also a methodical, systematic operation of renunciation, of 'purification'. One thinks of the *aphaeresis* of the Platonists, the movement of subtraction whereby God is reached at the end of a series of negations, as when in abolishing depth one passes from volume to surface, in negating breadth one passes from surface to line, and in cancelling length one proceeds from line to point. Working to impoverish literary language is not the mark of a 'withdrawal of being' and an 'inscription of words in nothingness', as existential or philosophizing criticism would like to have us believe. On the contrary, it is to work towards autonomous form, self-generated by the mathematical matrix and attaining a kind of abstractive purity. Beckett invents an always unfinished literary form that exists only in as much as it is (in his words) 'a form in motion'.

It was doubtless in *Worstward Ho* that Beckett achieved full mastery of his literary enterprise and attained 'victory over the reality of disorder'. A poetic art that announces both what it does and how it does it, and which elaborates in practice the theory (and practice) of literary abstraction, *Worstward Ho* totalizes the set of Beckett's innovations and discoveries.

The very movement of the text, what it 'recounts', is the process of 'abstractification': unlike the image in painting, the abstract literary image only exists in the movement of its very dissolution, in the progressive retreat of the meaning of words. Pejoration is not a philosophical or metaphysical intention or posture, but a means, peculiar to language, of achieving abstraction.

The limit to the process of 'abstractification' is set by the celebrated dependence of the word on a referent – which explains the good fortune of painters and musicians, so often referred to by Beckett, who were in a position to free sound and image from the conventions of signification or representation. Drawing the consequences of the difference between his material – words – and that of the other arts, Beckett fixed on an astounding solution which, although radical and unprecedented, is still 'shaky' because it stands in the constitutive uncertainty of the ambiguity of language. Beckett registers the impossibility of completely 'dissolving' the inevitable bond between word and thing and announces the kind of compromise that is the unsound rule of 'somehow on': he 'abstractifies' language as much as possible, to the point where there is 'nohow on'.

The abstract writer does not naively organize a pure, empty form. He only accomplishes his formal revolution by coming to terms with the necessary, 'uncancellable' bond between language and the world. Or rather, he invents abstract art in literature by striving and moving towards an impossible extinction of meaning.

Conclusion

Among the Deepening Shades

Beckett's consecration, at least in France, was not only an enormous misunderstanding. By appropriating his oeuvre, devotees of literature condemned him to silence and to the punishment suffered by the misunderstood in the Purgatory of ill seen, ill read writers.

Beckett was an iconoclast in the strict sense: he fought against literary academicism by producing an anti-literary literature. Yet it is in the name of profundity and existential pathos that he has been recognized and established as one of the twentieth century's greatest writers. Almost by definition, literary conservatism, but especially the aesthetic categories through which readers habitually apprehend run-of-the-mill literature, prevent his enterprise – one of the most subversive ever attempted – being understood. Mathematical formalism in literature is so detrimental to credos of poetic 'profundity' and ontological revelation that Beckett's oeuvre has had the most hackneyed idea of poetry – one he spent his whole life rejecting – applied to it, as if it were the quintessential embodiment of that idea.

Yet Beckett accomplished a revolution in literature that was as radical as Kandinsky's, or even, of a different nature, Duchamp's in art. His project of a genuinely autonomous literature, freed from the imperatives of representation and respecting only the principle of a combinatory of elements that has broken virtually any link with reality (or the conventions thought to represent reality), and the elaboration of a novel literary syntax, are on a par with the great aesthetic ruptures of the twentieth century. But his invention of literary abstraction has never truly been acknowledged. No doubt that is why he has remained without descendants: the quietus he delivered to literary realism literally went unnoticed. As a writer, he has not really acceded to existence because he has not been perceived: *non esse est non percipi*, as he would have said.

This challenge to the foundations of literature could only be mounted by a writer who all his life put himself in impossible literary situations. Probably no one has occupied so many reputedly untenable positions; no one has been attached to so many impossible aesthetics. To create an upheaval worthy of Joyce without following him on the path of the 'apotheosis of the word' compelled Beckett to think that very constraint and inaugurate a different branch of literary modernity, the 'literature of the unword'.

But to the very end, up until to his final pieces, he would leave room for the most intimate and pathetic, for naked images which, like motifs, remain fleeting, fragile, and all the more poignant in that they are always on the point of fading: the traces of his childhood, memories of his father, endlessly 'walk[ing] the roads', and the appearance of a woman '[w]ith those unseeing eyes I so begged when alive to look at me'.[1]

And at the end of this journey, nothing is more moving than to discover in the plays for television of the 1970s a text entitled '. . . but the clouds . . .', referring to a long poem by Yeats, 'The Tower' – a meditation on the figure of the poet, his memory, and the indelible images of the dead:

> Now I shall make my soul,
> Compelling it to study
> In a learned school
> Till the wreck of body,
> Slow decay of blood,
> Testy delirium
> Or dull decrepitude,
> Or what worse evil come –
> The death of friends, or death
> Of every brilliant eye
> That made a catch in the breath –
> Seem but the clouds of the sky
> When the horizon fades;
> Or a bird's sleepy cry
> Among the deepening shades.[2]

As if, at the end of one of the most improbable oeuvres of the twentieth century, Beckett, having finally arrived at a serene view of Ireland, had set about re-reading the Irish poet against whom he had struggled most, discovering in him something of a shared poetry, like a memory . . .

Notes

Introduction

1 Beckett, as Casanova records, found something of his own sense of being a superfluous man, his 'existence by proxy', reflected in Berkeley's idealist abolition of matter, which supposedly strikes at the idea of a solidly based world and thus parallels Beckett's own sense of estrangement. He thus reads his predecessor as some kind of sceptic, apparently unaware that Berkeley's idealism is among other things the reaction of a conservative Anglican cleric to the dangerously sceptical potentials of English empiricism.

2 See Perry Anderson, 'Modernity and Revolution', *New Left Review* 14, (March–April, 1984).

Preface

1 Maurice Blanchot, 'Où maintenant? Qui maintenant?', *Nouvelle revue française*, 1 October 1953; reprinted in Blanchot, *Le Livre à venir* (Paris: Gallimard, 1959), p. 312.

2 Samuel Beckett, *Endgame* (London: Faber and Faber, 1976), p. 29.

3 Blanchot, *Le Livre à venir*, p. 312.

4 In 1970 there were already 60 books and more than 5,000 articles devoted to Beckett's work, the overwhelming majority of them in English. Specialist publications are increasingly numerous and readers can now refer to the *Journal of Beckett Studies* (edited by S. E. Gontarsky and published in London by John Calder) and the bilingual journal *Samuel Beckett Today/aujourd'hui* (edited by Marius Bruning and Sjef Houpermans and published by Rodopi in Amsterdam), which lists all publications by and on Beckett.

Chapter 1: Ars Combinatoria

1 The very year of the production of *En Attendant Godot* in Paris and the publication of *L'Innommable* (Paris: Minuit, 1953), Maurice Blanchot published

his famous article 'Où maintenant? Qui maintenant?', which immediately installed Beckett in the pantheon of twentieth-century classics.

2 See Bruno Clément, *L'oeuvre sans qualités. Rhétorique de Samuel Beckett* (Paris: Seuil, 1994), p. 103 ff. (here p. 111).

3 Samuel Beckett, *Worstward Ho* (London: John Calder, 1999), p. 7. Given the extreme obscurity of this text, which I obviously cannot quote in full, if readers wish to verify the relevance of my analysis, they will have to consult the book, so as to follow the detail of my demonstration.

4 My emphasis.

5 Samuel Beckett, *Le Monde et le Pantalon* (Paris: Editions de Minuit, 1989), p. 28.

6 See James Knowlson, 'Pour une vraie biographie de Beckett', *Critique*, nos 519–520, August/September 1990, p. 655.

7 Michel Foucault, *The Order of Things* (London: Tavistock, 1977), pp. 14–15.

8 This is the word Beckett uses in connection with Proust's oeuvre, in an analysis written in Paris in 1930: see Samuel Beckett, *Proust and Three Dialogues* (London: John Calder, 1999).

Chapter 2: Youth and Genesis

1 Robert Pinget, 'Notre ami Sam', *Revue d'esthétique*, special issue on Samuel Beckett, Privat, Paris 1986; supplemented and republished (Paris: Jean-Michel Place, 1990), pp. vii–viii.

2 John Fletcher, 'Ecrivain bilingue', *Cahiers de l'Herne*, no. 31, *Samuel Beckett*, 1976, p. 211.

3 E. M. Cioran, *Cahiers de l'Herne*, no. 31, p. 49.

4 Bruno Clément, *L'oeuvre sans qualités. Rhétorique de Samuel Beckett* (Paris: Éditions du Seuil, 1994), pp. 374–5.

5 I.e. 'errors or omissions excepted'.

6 See Lawrence Harvey, *Samuel Beckett: Poet and Critic* (Princeton: Princeton University Press, 1970), pp. 296–8.

7 James Joyce, *A Portrait of the Artist as a Young Man* (New York: Viking Press, 1964), pp. 246–7.

8 Samuel Beckett, *More Pricks than Kicks* (London: Calder and Boyars, 1970), p. 53. One of Beckett's first works of fiction, it was published in London in 1934.

9 See, for example, James Joyce, 'James Clarence Mangan', in *The Critical Writings of James Joyce*, eds Ellsworth Mason and Richard Ellmann (London: Faber and Faber), 1959, p. 176.

10 Sean O'Casey, *Inishfallen, Fare Thee Well* (London: Pan, 1972), p. 89.

11 Samuel Beckett, *Dream of Fair to Middling Women*, quoted in Harvey, *Samuel Beckett*, p. 338.

12 See Harvey, *Samuel Beckett*, p. 297.

13 See Samuel Beckett, 'Recent Irish Poetry', in *Disjecta: Miscellaneous Writings and a Dramatic Fragment*, ed. and introd. Ruby Cohn (London: John Calder, 1983), pp. 70–76.

14 Beckett, 'Recent Irish Poetry', p. 70.

15 Beckett, 'Recent Irish Poetry', p. 70.

16 Cf. Declan Kiberd, *Inventing Ireland: The Literature of the Modern Nation* (Cambridge, MA and London, England: Harvard University Press, 1996).

17 Beckett, 'Recent Irish Poetry', p. 71.

18 Ibid., p. 70.

19 See below, pp. 40–41, 46–49.

20 Samuel Beckett, 'Censorship in the Saorstat', in *Disjecta*, pp. 84–8.

21 Samuel Beckett, 'The Essential and the Incidental', in *Disjecta*, pp. 82–3.

22 'The Essential and the Incidental', p. 82. *Juno and the Paycock*, which was performed in 1924, was an enormous success. The play was greeted by Yeats as 'a new hope and a new life for the theatre'. It remained at the base of the Abbey's repertoire.

23 James Joyce, *Ulysses* (Penguin: Harmondsworth 1975), p. 13.

24 See Clancy Sigal, 'Is This the Person to Murder Me?', *Sunday Times* (colour magazine), 1 March 1964, pp. 17–22. This remark presupposes that Beckett had a strong Irish accent readily identifiable by Londoners. This was confirmed to me by his English publisher, John Calder, during an interview.

25 '*Lady Windermere's Fan* took London by storm. In the tradition of the Irish writers of comedy that now runs from the days of Sheridan and Goldsmith to Bernard Shaw, Wilde became, like them, *court jester to the English*.': James Joyce, 'Oscar Wilde, Poet of *Salome*', in *The Critical Writings of James Joyce*, p. 202 (my emphasis). In the eighteenth century, Congreve, and then his successors Farquhar, Goldsmith and Sheridan, all of Irish origin, were to become famous in the comic genre.

26 George Bernard Shaw, letter of 11 June 1921 to Sylvia Beach, quoted in Richard Ellmann, *James Joyce*, new and revised edition (Oxford University Press: Oxford 1983), pp. 506–7.

27 Samuel Beckett, *Murphy* (London: John Calder, 1977), p. 116.

28 Beckett, *Murphy*, p. 69.

29 Beckett, *Murphy*, pp. 51, 53.

30 Beckett, *Murphy*, p. 28.

31 A. J. Leventhal, 'Les années trente', *Cahiers de l'Herne*, no. 31, p. 60.

32 Beckett, *Murphy*, p. 151.

33 Beckett, *Murphy*, p. 45; my emphasis.

34 Beckett, *Murphy*, p. 157.

35 Deirdre Bair, *Samuel Beckett: A Biography* (London: Jonathan Cape, 1978), p. 57.

36 Beckett, *Disjecta*, p. 19.

37 In his preface Philippe Soupault gives it to be understood that the 'the initial attempt made by Samuel Beckett, an Irishman who is a reader at the École normale . . . helped in this task by Alfred Péron, university graduate', had been largely revised and changed. See Soupault, 'A propos de la traduction d'*Anna Livia Plurabelle*', *Finnegans Wake*, passages/fragments adapted by André du Bouchet, followed by *Anna Livia Plurabelle* (Paris: Gallimard, 1962), pp. 87–8.

38 Bair, *Samuel Beckett*, pp. 129–30. Putnam accepted four of Beckett's poems for his anthology of young European poetry translated into English: *The European*

Caravan, edited by Madia Castelhun Darnton, George Reavey and Jacob Bronowski, part one (France, Spain, England and Ireland), published by Carren and Putnam in New York in 1931.

39 See Bair, *Samuel Beckett*, p. 275.

40 James Joyce, 'An Irish Poet', in *The Critical Writings of James Joyce*, p. 85.

41 James Joyce, 'The Day of the Rabblement', in *The Critical Writings of James Joyce*, pp. 70–1.

42 See John Kelly, 'The Irish Review', *L'année 1913: Les Formes esthétique de l'oeuvre d'art à la veille de la Première Guerre Mondiale*, ed. L. Brion-Guerry, (Paris: Klincksieck, 1971), p. 1024. See also Luke Gibbons, 'Constructing the Canon: Versions of National Identity', in S. Deane, A. Carpenter and J. Williams (eds), *The Field Day Anthology of Irish Writing* (Dublin: Field Day Publications, 1991), vol. III, pp. 950–55.

43 Cyril Connolly, *Enemies of Promise* (London: André Deutsch, 1973), p. 70.

44 *Libération*, 24 November 1988.

45 Joyce, 'The Day of the Rabblement', p. 71.

46 As a Catholic from a badly-off family, Joyce was not able to go to Trinity College Dublin.

47 In 1950 he translated an anthology of Mexican poems selected by Octavio Paz. The volume came out in 1958 under the title *Anthology of Mexican Poetry*.

48 Brian Inglis, *West Briton* (London: Faber, 1962), p. 122.

49 O'Casey, *Inishfallen, Fare Thee Well*, p. 24.

50 See Ellmann, *James Joyce*, p. 75.

51 See Harvey, *Samuel Beckett*, p. 187.

52 Samuel Beckett, 'Dante . . . Bruno. Vico . . . Joyce', in *Disjecta*, pp. 28, 26–7.

53 Beckett, *Disjecta*, p. 30.

54 We will find echoes of this assertion in Beckett's piece written (in English) for the BBC in 1956, *All That Fall*: '. . . sometimes one would think you were struggling with a dead language . . . Well, you know, it will be dead in time, just like our own poor dear Gaelic'. See Samuel Beckett, *All That Fall* (London: Faber and Faber, 1975), p. 35.

55 Beckett, *Disjecta*, p. 30; and see Dante, *De vulgari eloquentia*, ed. and trans. Steven Botterill (Cambridge: Cambridge University Press, 1996), pp. 11–13: 'For whoever is so misguided as to think that the place of his birth is the most delightful spot under the sun may also believe that his own language – his mother tongue, that is – is pre-eminent among all others . . . To me, however, the whole world is a homeland . . .'

56 Beckett, *Disjecta*, p. 30.

57 Jacques Le Goff, *The Birth of Purgatory*, trans. Arthur Goldhammer (London: Scolar Press), 1984, pp. 193–4.

58 Le Goff, *The Birth of Purgatory*, p. 198.

59 See Le Goff, *The Birth of Purgatory*, p. 200.

60 Le Goff, *The Birth of Purgatory*, p. 199.

61 In 1921 he declared to Arthur Power, 'you are an Irishman and you must write in your own tradition. Borrowed styles are no good . . . For myself, I always write about Dublin, because if I can get to the heart of Dublin I can

get to the heart of all the cities of the world': quoted in Ellmann, *James Joyce*, p. 505.

62 Beckett, *Disjecta*, p. 33.

63 Following, in particular, Sean O'Faolain, who devoted a short story to *Lough Derg*, and Patrick Kavanagh.

64 See Seamus Heaney, *Station Island* (London: Faber, 1984).

65 Dante, *The Divine Comedy. 2: Purgatorio*, trans. John D. Sinclair (New York: Oxford University Press, 1980), Canto IV, ll. 31–9, p. 59.

66 See below, pp. 61–62.

67 Beckett, *Disjecta*, p. 19.

68 *Purgatorio*, Canto IV, ll. 103–26, pp. 61–3. Cf. Ludovic Janvier, *Pour Samuel Beckett* (Paris: Éditions de Minuit, 1966), p. 102.

69 *Purgatorio*, Canto IV, ll. 95–9, p. 61.

70 See Walter A. Strauss, 'Le Belacqua de Dante et les clochards de Beckett', *Cahiers de l'Herne*, no. 31, 1976, pp. 295–315; Alfred Simon, *Beckett*, (Paris: Belfond, 1989), pp. 69–71; and Ruby Cohn, 'A Note on Beckett, Dante and Geulincx', *Comparative Literature*, no. XII, Winter 1960, pp. 93–4.

71 *Purgatorio*, Canto XX, l. 28.

72 Beckett, *More Pricks than Kicks*, p. 47.

73 Beckett, *Murphy*, pp. 47–8.

74 Samuel Beckett, *Company* (London: John Calder, 1996), p. 85.

75 See above, pp. 29–32. The poem is quoted in full on p. 30.

76 See, for example, *Purgatorio*, Canto XXIX, ll. 121–6 (p. 383): 'Three ladies came dancing in a round at the right wheel, one so red that she would hardly have been noted in the fire, another as if the flesh and bones had been of emerald, the third seeming new-fallen snow . . .'

77 See Harvey, *Samuel Beckett*, pp. 296–7.

Chapter 3: Philosophical Motifs

1 Samuel Beckett, letters to Thomas McGreevy of 7 June 1937 and Arland Usher of 15 June 1937; quoted by Deirdre Bair, in *Samuel Beckett: A Biography* (London: Jonathan Cape, 1978), p. 258.

2 Samuel Beckett, letter to Georges Reavey of 8 October 1932, quoted by Bair, in *Samuel Beckett*, p. 155.

3 Samuel Beckett, letter to Thomas McGreevy of 6 October 1937, quoted in Bair, *Samuel Beckett*, p. 265.

4 Samuel Beckett, letter to Mary Manning Howe of 17 June 1937, quoted in Bair, *Samuel Beckett*, p. 251.

5 These poems would be published in 1935 at their author's expense by George Reavey at Europa Press, under the title *Echo's Bones and Other Precipitates*.

6 In *Molloy*, which is also a circular bike ride around an island from which there is no escape, Beckett would remember it.

7 Quoted in Lawrence Harvey, *Samuel Beckett: Poet and Critic* (Princeton: Princeton University Press, 1970), p. 118.

8 Harvey, *Samuel Beckett*, p. 273.

9 Harvey, *Samuel Beckett*, p. 222.

10 Samuel Beckett, *Krapp's Last Tape* and *Embers* (London: Faber and Faber, 1976), p. 18.

11 Samuel Beckett, *Waiting for Godot* (London: Faber and Faber 1977), p. 9.

12 Arnold Geulincx (1624–69), a Flemish philosopher and follower of Descartes and Malebranche, who introduced Descartes into Holland.

13 Arnold Geulincx, *Ethics*, book III, quoted by Alain de Lattre, *L'Occasionalisme d'Arnold Geulincx* (Paris: Éditions de Minuit, 1967), p. 534.

14 Samuel Beckett, *Molloy/Malone Dies/The Unnamable* (London: John Calder, 1976), p. 51.

15 Geulincx, *Ethics*, book III, quoted by de Lattre, *L'Occasionalisme d'Arnold Geulincx*, p. 568.

16 de Lattre, *L'Occasionalisme d'Arnold Geulincx*, p. 569.

17 Samuel Beckett, *Murphy* (London: John Calder 1977), p. 48; my emphasis.

18 Samuel Beckett, *More Pricks than Kicks* (London: Calder and Boyars, 1970), p. 41.

19 Samuel Beckett, *Dream of Fair to Middling Women*, in Beckett, *Disjecta*, p. 49.

20 Samuel Beckett, 'The End', in *Collected Shorter Prose 1945–1980* (London: John Calder, 1986), p. 70.

21 Beckett, *More Pricks than Kicks*, p. 39.

22 See Harvey, *Samuel Beckett*, p. 319 and Bair, *Samuel Beckett*, pp. 164–5.

23 Beckett, *Murphy*, p. 64.

24 Ibid., pp. 6, 142.

25 Ibid., p. 101, my emphasis.

26 See Gilles Deleuze, 'L'épuisé', in Samuel Beckett, *Quad et autres pieces pour la television*, trans. Edith Fournier (Paris: Éditions de Minuit, 1992), p. 95.

27 Beckett, *Murphy*, pp. 63, 66.

28 Ibid., p. 64.

29 Ibid.

30 Ibid.

31 Beckett, *Murphy*, p. 63.

32 Samuel Beckett, letter to George Reavey of 6 August 1937, quoted in Eoin O'Brien, *The Beckett Country* (Dublin: Black Cat Press, 1986), p. 308.

33 Samuel Beckett, *Eleutheria*, trans. Michael Brodsky (New York: Foxrock, 1995), p. 191.

34 Beckett, *Molloy/Malone Dies/The Unnamable*, p. 66.

35 Samuel Beckett, 'Le calmant', *Nouvelles et textes pour rien* (Paris: Editions de Minuit, 1958), p. 45. [This sentence does not feature in Beckett's own translation of his text published as *The Calmative*. Trs.]

36 Tinkers, commonplace in Ireland at the beginning of the twentieth century, had acquired their literary credentials thanks, among others, to the dramatic oeuvre of J. M. Synge (1871–1909) and had in a sense become 'classic' characters of the national literature. In their way, Beckett's tramps also belong to this Irish literary tradition.

37 Samuel Beckett, 'The End', *Collected Shorter Prose*, p. 70.

38 Beckett, *Collected Shorter Prose*, p. 60.
39 Ibid., p. 62.
40 Ibid., p. 68.
41 Ibid., p. 70.
42 Ibid., p. 65.
43 Ibid., pp. 65–6.
44 Ibid., pp. 63–4.
45 Following the same logic, Yeats, having closely read the work of Berkeley and the eighteenth-century Anglo-Irish in 1925, pronounced himself the enemy of the 'materialist philosophy of Newton, Locke and Hobbes' (quoted in René Fréchet, *W. B. Yeats*, Aubier, Paris 1975, p. 35).
46 Beckett, *Murphy*, p. 138.
47 See Gilles Deleuze, 'The Greatest Irish Film', in *Essays Critical and Clinical*, trans. Daniel W. Smith and Michael A. Greco (London: Verso, 1998), p. 23.
48 Deleuze, *Essays Critical and Clinical*, p. 26.
49 Deleuze, *Essays Critical and Clinical*, p. 23.
50 Harvey, *Samuel Beckett*, p. 247.
51 Samuel Beckett, *Film* (screenplay) (London: Faber and Faber, 1972), p. 11. Directed by Alan Schneider and starring Buster Keaton, *Film* was made in 1964.
52 Beckett, *Film*, p. 11.
53 Beckett, *Film*, p. 31.
54 Deleuze, *Essays Critical and Clinical*, p. 26.
55 Cf., among others, Tzvetan Todorov, 'L'espoir chez Beckett', *Revue d'esthétique*, special issue on Samuel Beckett, Privat, Paris 1986, pp. 27–36 and Peter Murphy, 'The Nature of Allegory in "The Lost Ones", or the Quincunx Realistically Considered', *Journal of Beckett Studies*, no. 7, Spring 1982, pp. 71–88.
56 Antoinette Weber-Caflisch, *Chacun son Dépeupleur. Sur Samuel Beckett* (Paris: Éditions de Minuit, 1994), pp. 65, 36.
57 Alain Badiou, *Beckett, l'increvable désir* (Paris: Hachette, 1995), p. 49.
58 Beckett, *Murphy*, p. 65.
59 Beckett, 'The Lost Ones', in *Collected Shorter Prose 1945–1980* (London: John Calder, 1986), p. 161.
60 Beckett, *Collected Shorter Prose*, p. 167.
61 Beckett, *Collected Shorter Prose*, p. 177.
62 This would suggest another meaning of the French title: the 'depleter' is the place where the disappearance of any desire and any sexual activity would lead to the extinction of the human race – a 'depopulation'.
63 Blaise Pascal, *Pensées*, XXV, 641, trans. A. J. Krailsheimer (Harmondsworth: Penguin, 1983), p. 238.
64 Weber-Caflisch, *Chacun son Dépeupleur*, p. 18.
65 Badiou, *Beckett*, pp. 49–50.
66 Beckett, *Collected Shorter Prose*, p. 161.
67 Beckett, *Collected Shorter Prose*, p. 176.
68 See *Collected Shorter Prose*, pp. 174–5.
69 Beckett, *Collected Shorter Prose*, p. 177.

70 A full account of this text would require reference to Swift's *Gulliver's Travels* and its inverted utopia, especially in order to understand Beckett's geographical and mathematical specifications.

71 Beckett, *Collected Shorter Prose*, pp. 177–8.

Chapter 4: The Invention of Abstract Literature

1 Samuel Beckett, letter to Thomas McGreevy of 22 December 1937, cited in Deirdre Bair, *Samuel Beckett: A Biography* (London: Jonathan Cape, 1978), pp. 271–2.

2 *Les Temps Modernes*, no. 14, 1946, pp. 288–93.

3 Lawrence Harvey, *Samuel Beckett: Poet and Critic* (Princeton: Princeton University Press, 1970), pp. 183–4.

4 Harvey, *Samuel Beckett*, p. 183.

5 Samuel Beckett, letter to George Reavey of 14 May 1947, quoted in Bair, *Samuel Beckett*, p. 364.

6 Samuel Beckett, *Krapp's Last Tape* and *Embers* (London: Faber and Faber, 1976), p. 18.

7 See Deirdre Bair, 'La vision, enfin', *Cahiers de l'Herne*, no. 31, *Samuel Beckett*, 1976, pp. 63–72.

8 Beckett, *Krapp's Last Tape* and *Embers*, pp. 15–16.

9 Preserved in the Humanities Research Center, University of Texas at Austin.

10 Samuel Beckett, letter to Marthe Arnaud and Bram Van Velde of 25 March 1952, J. Putnam archives, quoted in *Bram Van Velde*, (Paris: Éditions du Centre Pompidou, 1989), p. 175.

11 Beckett, *Le Monde et le Pantalon*, p. 33.

12 Samuel Beckett, *Le Monde et le Pantalon* (Paris: Éditions de Minuit, 1989), p. 36.

13 Beckett, *Le Monde et le Pantalon*, p. 33.

14 Beckett, *Le Monde et le Pantalon*, p. 9.

15 Beckett, *Le Monde et le Pantalon*, pp. 11–12.

16 Samuel Beckett, 'Les peintres de l'empêchement', in *Disjecta*, pp. 135–6.

17 Beckett, 'Les peintres de l'empêchement', p. 136.

18 See Samuel Beckett, 'German Letter of 1937', in *Disjecta*, pp. 52–3.

19 Beckett, *Le Monde et le Pantalon*, p. 28.

20 See Harvey, *Samuel Beckett*, p. 249.

21 By means of subtle comparisons Beckett accused the Surrealists of being 'charming obscurantist[s]': 'Les peintres de l'empêchement', p. 135.

22 Beckett, 'Les peintres de l'empêchement', p. 137; my emphasis.

23 Beckett, *Le Monde et le Pantalon*, p. 21.

24 Marcelin Pleynet, 'Le musée-galerie, Bram Van Velde', *Art International*, vol. 15, no. 2, pp. 46–8.

25 See Samuel Beckett, 'Three Dialogues', in *Disjecta*, pp. 138–45. Georges Duthuit was Matisse's son-in-law. An art critic, he was close to Nicolas de Staël, Alberto Giacometti, Pierre Tal Coat, André Masson and so forth, and rubbed shoulders with André du Bouchet, Georges Bataille and René Char.

26 Beckett, 'Three Dialogues', p. 139.
27 Beckett, 'Three Dialogues', p. 142.
28 Beckett, 'Three Dialogues', p. 145.
29 Beckett, *Krapp's Last Tape* and *Embers*, p. 16.
30 Samuel Beckett, letter to Thomas McGreevy of 13 March 1948, quoted in Bair, *Samuel Beckett*, p. 374.
31 Harvey, *Samuel Beckett*, p. 248.
32 Harvey, *Samuel Beckett*, p. 249.
33 See Maurice Blanchot, 'La disparition de la littérature' and 'Le livre à venir', in *Le Livre à venir*, pp. 285, 334.
34 See Blanchot, 'Où maintenant? Qui maintenant?', p. 316.
35 See Blanchot, 'La recherche du point zéro', in *Le Livre à venir*, p. 306.
36 Blanchot, 'La recherche du point zéro', p. 306.
37 Blanchot, 'La disparition de la littérature', p. 292.
38 Rainer Michael Mason notes that 'the Beckett effect [i.e. what he considered as such] had from 1945 set critics on an (endless) road excluding the formalist approach: Bram Van Velde was painting the impossibility of painting, and any philology was therefore futile': 'La croissance d'un arbre: notes sur l'individuation du style de Bram Van Velde', in *Bram Van Velde*, p. 40.
39 Harvey, *Samuel Beckett*, p. 249.
40 Ludovic Janvier, *Pour Samuel Beckett* (Paris: Éditions de Minuit, 1966), p. 257.
41 Tom F. Driver, 'Beckett by the Madeleine', *Columbia University Forum*, 1961, p. 23.
42 Harvey, *Samuel Beckett*, p. 249.
43 Beckett, 'Dante . . . Bruno. Vico . . . Joyce', in *Disjecta*, p. 27.
44 Beckett, *Molloy/Malone Dies/The Unnamable*, p. 293.
45 The centrality of paradox in Beckett has of course been commented on extensively by critics (see, in particular, Raymond Federman, 'Le paradoxe du menteur', *Cahiers de l'Herne*, no. 31, 1976, pp. 148–66).
46 Beckett, *Molloy/Malone Dies/The Unnamable*, p. 316.
47 See Janvier, *Pour Samuel Beckett*, p. 257; and see also Olga Bernal, *Le Monde*, 17 January 1968.
48 Beckett, *Molloy/Malone Dies/The Unnamable*, p. 296.
49 Samuel Beckett, *How It Is* (London: John Calder, 1977), p. 7.
50 Samuel Beckett, *Company* (London: John Calder, 1996), pp. 7–9.
51 Beckett, *Molloy/Malone Dies/The Unnamable*, p. 305.
52 Samuel Beckett, 'The Image', in *As the Story Was Told* (London: John Calder, and New York: Riverrun Press, 1990), p. 39.
53 This refusal has sometimes been described as 'de-metaphorization'. Cf. Declan Kiberd, *Inventing Ireland: The Literature of a Modern Nation* (London: Jonathan Cape 1995), p. 458.
54 Harvey, *Samuel Beckett*, pp. 249–50.
55 Beckett, *Le Monde et le Pantalon*, p. 28.
56 Samuel Beckett, *Worstward Ho* (London: John Calder, 1999), p. 10.
57 Beckett, *Le Monde et le Pantalon*, p. 30.

58 According to Robert Creeley, who has recounted one of his conversations with Beckett, 'It was his dream to realize one word that was absolutely self-created': J. C. C. Mays, 'Samuel Beckett (1907–1989)', *The Field Day Anthology of Irish Writing*, ed. S. Deane, A. Carpenter and J. Williams (Derry: Field Day Publications, 1991), vol. III, p. 237.

59 Beckett arrived in Paris at the end of October 1937 (cf. Bair, *Samuel Beckett*, p. 265).

60 Translation of Beckett, 'German Letter of 1937', in *Disjecta*, pp. 171–2.

61 Beckett, 'German Letter of 1937', p. 172.

62 Ibid., p. 173.

63 Beckett, *Watt*, p. 78.

64 Beckett, *Molloy/Malone Dies/The Unnamable*, p. 50.

65 This is why Bruno Clément can speak of an 'auto-textuality' in Beckett – that is, constant citation and reprises of the oeuvre in the oeuvre: *L'oeuvre sans qualités*, p. 382 ff.

66 Jérôme Lindon's testimony in the 'Avertissement' to *Eleuthéria* (Paris: Éditions de Minuit, 1995, p. 7) is explicit in this respect: 'Samuel Beckett was always very hard on his old works and initially even deemed unpublishable an oeuvre that he ended up, at the insistence of his friends, translating or delivering to the printer'.

67 See Bair, *Samuel Beckett*, p. 383.

68 Beckett, *Le Monde et le Pantalon*, p. 31.

69 Janvier, *Pour Samuel Beckett*, p. 241.

70 Quoted in Harvey, *Samuel Beckett*, p. 249.

71 Harvey, *Samuel Beckett*, p. 267.

72 Beckett, *Molloy/Malone Dies/The Unnamable*, pp. 327–9.

73 Beckett, 'German Letter of 1937', p. 171.

74 Harvey, *Samuel Beckett*, p. 196; my emphasis.

75 Quoted by Lawrence Graver, *Samuel Beckett: Waiting for Godot* (Cambridge: Cambridge University Press, 1989), p. 6.

76 See Graver, *Samuel Beckett*, p. 6.

77 Beckett, *Disjecta*, p. 47.

78 Apart from *Acte sans paroles I* (1956) and *Acte sans paroles II* (1959), descriptions of mimes; various sketches from the 1960s that were never finished; *Cascando* (1962), written for the French broadcasting service at the request of Marcel Mihalovici; and *Catastrophe* (1982), dedicated to Vaclav Havel, who was imprisoned at the time.

79 This list has been established following Edith Fournier, 'Liste chronologique des oeuvres de Samuel Beckett', in *Revue d'esthétique*, special issue on Samuel Beckett, Privat, Paris 1986, pp. 416–23. *Ghost Trio, But the Clouds, Radio I and II*, and *Quad* were not translated into French by Beckett.

80 Quoted in Bair, *Samuel Beckett*, p. 381.

81 Samuel Beckett, letter to Thomas McGreevy of 14 December 1953, quoted in Bair, *Samuel Beckett*, p. 435.

82 Ludovic Janvier, 'Roman/théâtre', *Revue d'esthétique*, special issue on Samuel Beckett, Privat, Paris 1986, p. 48.

83 Melvin J. Friedman, among others, also notes the differentiated use of the two languages in Beckett – English as dramatic language and French as narrative language –in order to evoke an alteration of technique corresponding to a change of personality, mood, or genre: 'The Creative Writer as a Polyglot: Valery Larbaud and Samuel Beckett', *Transactions of the Wisconsin Academy of Sciences, Art and Letters*, XLIX, 1960, pp. 236–9.

84 J. C. C. Mays, 'Samuel Beckett (1906–89)', *The Field Day Anthology of Irish Writing*, vol. III, p. 235. For Eric Eigenmann, Beckett's dramatic texts 'rest on the paradox that they transgress what might seem to be the very conditions of theatre': 'Mise en scène de l'effacement', *Critique*, nos 519–520, August/September 1990, p. 688.

85 See, for example, the testimony of Rick Cluchey in Mays, 'Samuel Beckett', p. 236: 'tonally, he becomes a musician . . . He arrives at the point where he can tell you instantly if . . . the musicalization is incorrect'; and also that of Delphine Seyrig ('Haute précision', *Revue d'esthétique*, special issue on Samuel Beckett, Privat, Paris 1986): 'To play Beckett . . . you have to know how to speak and act mechanicall . . . He is like a conductor, he beats time.'

86 Janvier, 'Roman/théâtre', p. 254; my emphasis.

87 Roger Blin, 'Conversations avec Lynda Peskine', *Revue d'esthétique*, special issue on Beckett, Privat, Paris 1986, p. 164; my emphasis.

88 See Edith Fournier, 'Marcel Mihalovici et Samuel Beckett, musicians du retour', in *Revue d'esthétique*, special issue on Beckett, pp. 243–9.

89 Samuel Beckett, 'Quad', in *The Complete Dramatic Works* (London: Faber and Faber, 1986), pp. 452, 454.

90 Quoted by Rémi Labrusse, in 'Beckett et la peinture: Le témoignage d'une correspondance inédite', *Critique*, nos 519–520, August/September, p. 675.

91 Samuel Beckett, *Watt* (London: John Calder, 1978), p. 166.

92 Beckett, *Molloy/Malone Dies/The Unnamable*, p. 69.

93 See Edith Fournier, ' "Sans": cantate et fugue pour un refuge', *Les Lettres modernes*, September/October 1970, pp. 149–60; reprinted in *Critique*, nos 519–520, August/September 1990.

94 Samuel Beckett, 'Enough', in *Six Residua* (London: John Calder, 1978), pp. 26–7.

95 Beckett, *How It Is*, p. 41.

96 Samuel Beckett, letter to J. Putnam of 5 February 1957, Putnam archives, quoted in *Bram Van Velde* (Paris: Éditions du Centre Pompidou, 1989), p. 187.

Conclusion

1 Samuel Beckett, '. . . but the clouds . . .', in *Ends and Odds: Plays and Sketches* (London: Faber and Faber, 1977), pp. 56, 55.

2 W. B. Yeats, 'The Tower', in *Selected Poetry* (London: Pan/Macmillan, 1982), pp. 111–12.

DATE DUE

85037